Locomotion and Mechanics

Kevin McCombs

Cavendish Square
New York

Published in 2017 by Cavendish Square Publishing, LLC
243 5th Avenue, Suite 136, New York, NY 10016

Library of Congress Cataloging-in-Publication Data

Names: McCombs, Kevin, author.
Title: Locomotion and mechanics / Kevin McCombs.
Description: New York : Cavendish Square Publishing, [2017] | Series: Robotics
Identifiers: LCCN 2016025997 (print) | LCCN 2016026878 (ebook) | ISBN 9781502620262 (library bound) | ISBN 9781502619426 (E-book)
Subjects: LCSH: Robotics--Juvenile literature. | Robots--Design and construction--Juvenile literature.
Classification: LCC TJ211.2 .M3765 2017 (print) | LCC TJ211.2 (ebook) | DDC 629.8/92--dc23
LC record available at https://lccn.loc.gov/2016025997

Editorial Director: David McNamara
Editor: Fletcher Doyle
Copy Editor: Nathan Heidelberger
Associate Art Director: Amy Greenan
Designer: Alan Sliwinski
Production Coordinator: Karol Szymczuk
Photo Research: J8 Media

Printed in the United States of America

Contents

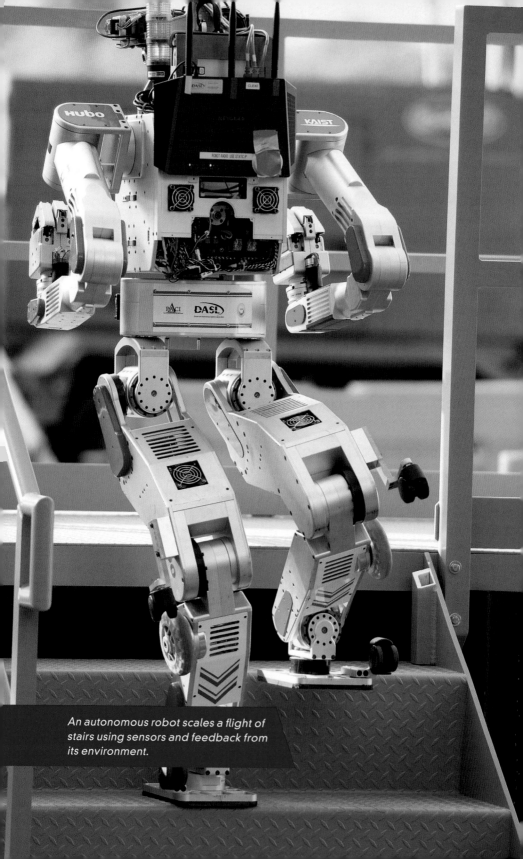

An autonomous robot scales a flight of stairs using sensors and feedback from its environment.

1

What Is a Robot Made Of?

Think back to when you were a young kid and you first saw a robot in a science fiction movie or television show. There's a good chance the robot looked like a boxy metal man who walked on stiff mechanical legs and spoke with a synthesized monotone voice. These kinds of "robots" are usually constructed by old mad scientists in some kind of lab using space-age tools and technology. As a result, robots are made to sound like arcane creations of near infinite complexity, requiring the engineering prowess of some reclusive robotics genius.

In the real world, however, robots rarely walk on two legs or are made to look like humanoids at all. In fact, they are constructed by everyday engineers, technicians, and curious students to perform a wide range of tasks for the society we live in. Robots help produce our electronics, cars, food, and much more using **locomotion** and mechanics to get consistent results from repetitive processes and motions. In this book, we will take a look at how people construct robots and robotic assemblies by breaking them down into simple systems and identifying the materials used to make those systems. The movements of a robot can be understood completely when looking at how each part moves in conjunction with the others. While robotic systems can indeed be works of great complexity and creativity, they all operate on the same fundamental principles of physics and utilize the movements of simple machines to create larger assemblies.

Our task in this chapter is to dispel a bit of the mystery behind the outer shell of a robot and introduce a few common robotic components to store in our mental toolkits. Additionally, we'll look at a number of raw materials used to fabricate robot parts along with their relative advantages and disadvantages. This should help you get a better sense of the kinds of movements robots are able to make with even an abbreviated list of mechanical components. Engineers and robot builders often utilize a small number of mechanical parts to achieve multiple tasks simply by coming up with creative solutions for attaching moving systems together. So let's get started and spark some ideas for mechanical movement.

Motors

As the title of this book suggests, we'll be looking at the way in which some robots move from one place to another, or locomotion. While certainly not the only available method, many robots move around using motors to spin wheels or position feet on the ground. You're probably familiar with the role that combustion engines play in a car or truck. An engine is a kind of motor that converts the energy of combusted gasoline into the mechanical rotation of a shaft. Robots rarely operate on combustion as a source of energy, opting for electrical, pneumatic, or elastic energy sources instead. Each style of conversion from potential energy into mechanical rotation can be effective for a number of applications. Let's look at a few of them.

Electric motors operate by taking energy from a battery or other electrical source and using that voltage to create electromagnetic force. In a direct current (DC) motor, the part that moves the shaft inside an electric motor is called a **rotor** and is usually lined with conductors that get voltage from the power source. Separated by a minor air gap, the rotor interacts with a **stator** that is comprised of wire windings or permanent magnets. As current flows through the conductors of the rotor, the electromagnetic stator changes poles that attract and repel the magnetic poles of the rotor, causing the rotor to flip end over end, thus creating a rotational force.

Simple Electric Motor

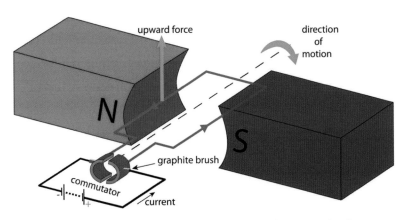

The interaction between electromagnetic fields produces rotation in a simple brushed DC motor.

There are many different kinds of rotor and stator configurations, but for the most part, we'll be dealing with DC electric motors for our robotic applications. One distinction to be made, however, is between brushed and **brushless DC motors**. A brushed DC motor utilizes two **commutators** to provide an electric current to the rotor. The commutators are comprised of a conductor and usually a spring that applies pressure to the brush on the rotor magnet. This keeps an electrical contact between the power source and the rotor even when the electromagnet is rotating by pressing the brushes against the surface. DC motor brushes do, however, wear out over time and can cause sparks from the contact with the electromagnet, making them less usable for industrial, long-term applications.

The brushless DC motor is structured a bit differently. The rotor is usually positioned on the *outside* of the stator and is made of one or many permanent magnets. The stator is made up of multiple coils in a circular array that energize at different times. When a stator coil becomes energized, it creates an electromagnetic field, which attracts or repels the poles of the magnet(s) on the rotor. If that coil turns off, and the coil right next to it energizes, the rotor will move to align its poles once again. If you can imagine the coils getting turned on and off quickly in order, the following alignment of the rotor's poles will cause the shaft to spin as it gets bumped around the ever-changing magnetic field.

In order to achieve this rapid switching process, brushless DC motors use special control circuitry to set the timing and pattern of the on and off cycles for each stator coil. At this

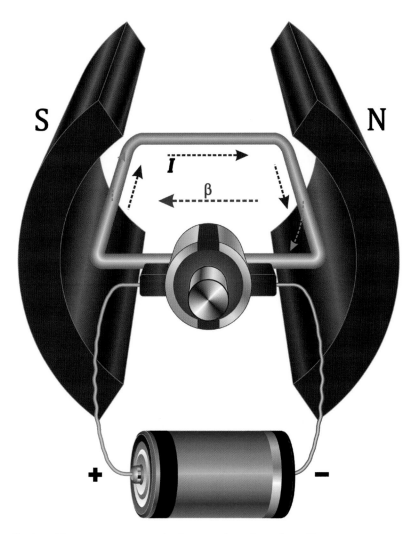

The brushless motor constantly changes the orientation of its electromagnetic field to produce rotation in its permanent magnets.

point, you might be wondering how the motor can tell that the coil that's being energized is in close enough proximity to the rotor that it will cause a movement around the circle. The brushless DC motor circuit often uses a device called a "Hall effect sensor" to measure changes in the electromagnetic field of the motor. This is extremely useful because it can help determine the position of the rotor based on the interaction between the rotating permanent magnets and the sensor. This sensor allows the controller to determine which coil to turn on at what time in order to ensure a smooth, continuous rotation of the motor. Brushless DC motors are very popular for robotics applications because they are highly energy efficient, have low noise, and operate reliably over long periods of time.

Pneumatic Motors

Pneumatic motors use compressed air or gas to spin a rotor in a housing that has a directional path for the air to escape. Using a stream of pressurized air as an energy source, a pneumatic motor has fins attached to the rotor that spin like a turbine. Pneumatic motors have selectable valves, which allow you to control the direction of the airflow and, consequently, the direction of the motor. These motors are seen most commonly in air tools like grinders or impact wrenches due to their reliability and performance. Due to the fact that there are generally no electric components on pneumatic motors, the motors stay much cooler under load, making them good for prolonged operation. Pneumatic motors, as opposed to other types of pneumatic devices, require a hefty amount of airflow to operate. This means that the air tank or compressor required to run them for extended periods must be sizeable, making them more ideal for large-scale robotic applications.

Clockwork Motors

Some motors use stored energy in springs or elastic materials to rotate when released. These motors are called "**clockwork motors**" due to their prominence in clocks, which rely on a wound spring mechanism to create movement. These motors require an initial winding force to operate. This must come either from another external motor or manual winding movement. These can be extremely useful for certain robotic mechanisms due to their simplicity and lack of direct need for electricity. Clockwork motors can be wound by other powered mechanical processes on a machine, making them versatile for tasks that are occasionally triggered or take a long time to execute before needing to be wound again.

Raw Materials

Robots can be made from a large variety of materials based on factors like strength, flexibility, cost, corrosion resistance, and many others. It's important to get an idea of the kinds of raw materials that are out there and that are commonly used to build robot parts. There's usually a tradeoff for using one material over another, which ultimately depends on the application at hand. Whether it's made of metal, plastics, or composites, robots are designed with these raw materials in mind to achieve certain goals.

Metals

Perhaps the most common metal used in robotics is aluminum. Aluminum is a lightweight, durable metal that does not rust or corrode over time. This metal is very machinable, meaning that it is easy to cut and shape relative to other metals like steel and titanium. While thin pieces of aluminum can be bent easily by human hands, the strength-to-weight ratio is very good for mechanisms under reasonable loads. Another important factor is that aluminum is nonmagnetic, making it safe to have around electronics that are sensitive to magnetic field interference. Aluminum, however, is very electrically conductive, meaning it should be properly insulated from electrical components to avoid short circuits.

This high-school competition robot frame is constructed of modular aluminum components.

Aluminum is usually around $0.70 per pound (0.45 kilograms), making it inexpensive to purchase as a raw material. There are also more modular aluminum products that are particularly good for robot construction. Extruded aluminum tubing called **80-20** uses a system of channels for easily connecting and mounting pieces. The 80-20 material is also great for mechanical components that need to slide in the channels, such as lifting mechanisms or mechanical actuators. Some aluminum stock comes with preexisting hole patterns for ease of connection at various angles. "Tetrix," "Matrix," and "Actobotics" are three kinds of aluminum with modular hole systems. These can be a fantastic place to start when looking to put together a robot frame or prototype mechanism. Simply bolt the pieces together and attach moving components!

Steel is also a very common building material for robots. As a reference, steel is about twice as heavy as aluminum, but roughly half the price per pound. Steel is structurally robust, so it is generally used for mechanisms that need to stay strong under great force. The weight of steel can also be used as an advantage if a mechanism is in need of counterbalancing or weight distribution. Steel is perhaps most popular as a construction material for buildings or large structures, but it certainly has a place in moving robotic components that need to be rock solid. Steel is both magnetic and susceptible to rust and other corrosion, however. As a result, steel should be properly coated in humid conditions and positioned intelligently around permanent magnets.

Titanium is a metal that is incredibly strong but incredibly expensive. Titanium is, in some cases, as strong as steel, but it is nowhere near as dense, making it a lightweight alternative. The cost, however, can be as high as $40 per pound for raw titanium, making it prohibitively expensive for some projects. Titanium is often used in aerospace applications like structural supports for rocket engines due to high heat capacity and strength without adding too much weight to the spacecraft.

Plastics

Plastics can be good for applications that don't require the strength or durability of metals, especially on small robotic systems. The physical properties of plastics such as coefficient of friction can also be attractive factors when selecting a material. (The coefficient of friction is the ratio between the force necessary to move one surface over another and the pressure between the two surfaces.) While some plastics are easily cut by hand tools, some special materials are machinable and can be used as a metal substitute for some parts. This is especially useful when you need parts that are non–electrically conductive for mounting circuits and microcontrollers.

Nylon is a common plastic material for small mechanisms and moving parts. While it is not the easiest material to cut due to fraying edges, it can make for good armatures or attachments on motors. Nylon is what's known as a thermoplastic, meaning it deforms at a certain temperature (around 420 to 500 degrees Fahrenheit, or 215 to 260 degrees Celsius) then solidifies into a shape when it cools. It's also noteworthy that nylon ropes and fishing line can be great for use on mechanical **pulley** assemblies or winch systems.

There are two special plastics known as **ABS** (acrylonitrile butadiene styrene) and PLA (polylactic acid) which are used in some robots. These plastics are particularly interesting because they are the most popular materials for 3-D printing. These plastics have a low melting point, around 170°F (77°C), making them good for extrusion (pressing or pushing out) through a heated nozzle. While these materials aren't very strong, they are great for rapid prototyping and disposable parts. Sheets of these materials are also fairly cheap, at around $1.50 per square foot (929 square centimeters) for sheets that are ⅛ inch (3 millimeters) thick. These plastic sheets are good for mounting electronics, creating enclosures, and creating small frames for some components.

"**Delrin**" (polyoxymethylene) is a strong, machinable plastic. This material is particularly valuable because of its low coefficient of friction. For robotics applications, this means that Delrin is a great candidate for sliding mechanisms. Delrin can be used to great effect in tandem with aluminum frame components to allow sliding motion between components. Additionally, Delrin makes for effective moving pieces like ball bearings or gears due to its dimensional stability.

Polycarbonates (or plexiglass) are another class of plastics that are widely used in robotics. This material is special because it can be transparent, making for great enclosures for control systems. Robot aesthetics often feature the inner workings of mechanisms and electronics. What better way to show off a robotic system than to surround its frame with see-through plates on all sides? As an added bonus, polycarbonates look amazing in tandem with LED light systems, which are also commonly used on robots.

A grid of LEDs behind a covering of plexiglass is used to produce images on a robotic assembly.

Composites

Composites are special materials made up of multiple layers that are sealed by an epoxy or resin. Composites generally have a very good strength-to-weight ratio as they are essentially chemically hardened pieces of strong cloth. The most common composite is fiberglass. This material has been used in a huge range of applications from surfboards to pressurized tanks due to its ability to conform to almost any moldable shape. Fiberglass is created by layering incredibly thin strands of glass on a mold or surface. These layers are then coated with a hardening resin that bonds the layers and adheres it to the form of the mold. The result is a structural, but thin, building material that can be nearly any shape imaginable.

In robotics, **carbon fiber** is a very useful composite because of the aforementioned strength-to-weight ratio. Layers of razor-thin carbon make for a material that is incredibly tough yet light as a feather. The drawback, however, is that carbon fiber is expensive to make, and even more expensive to buy. Sheets can be purchased commercially for about $55 per square foot. As a result of the steep price, carbon fiber is generally used where necessary in applications like drones where every ounce is critical for efficient flight.

Conclusion

In this chapter, we have looked briefly at motors and raw materials to gain some insight into the most basic components of a robot. While there are many other critical materials required to tackle a robot build, these categories are the true backbone of a locomotive system, providing both structure and rotation for movement. Motors and raw materials are the fundamental building blocks of robotics. In the next chapter, we will explore the concept of fitting components together to create working mechanisms. Now that we have shed light on some different kinds of motors and materials, we will be able to start making decisions about what kinds of parts we might need to build a given robotic system. With motors and a variety of different materials at our disposal, let's dive into making things move!

Robotic arms precisely weld metal pieces together on an assembly line.

2 Understanding Constraints

Now that we have looked at some basic raw materials used to make robots, our task in this chapter is to explore the inner workings of various kinds of mechanisms. We will go over how certain motions are performed by various systems and how engineers fit these systems together to make a whole robot. Robots can be works of great ingenuity and design, requiring that all systems move together seamlessly in places with very little space to spread out components. This chapter will look at some methods for calculating space requirements based on the movements of a mechanism. In addition, we will explore some other common design constraints like the operating temperature of components, wiring and cable management, and limiting the movements of some mechanisms with sensors and mechanical stops.

The first step for determining how mechanisms will fit together is identifying the task the robot is made to accomplish. Will this robot be lifting objects in a factory? Will it be stacking and sorting pieces on an assembly line?

Performing precise movements in a lab experiment? All of these engineering problems come with different sets of design constraints for precision, space, and size of components. Once we understand the physical and technical constraints of a project, we can begin to make decisions about the robot, such as the power and size of motors or the number of different moving stages of a mechanism.

For instance, a robot that welds car frames on a factory assembly line will often have to have numerous **axes of articulation** to reach the desired angles and spaces of a welded joint. You can think of these axes as being analogous to joints that contribute to the incredible number of ways you can move your own human arm. An articulation in the body is a joint for the purpose of motion. These joints work together to produce arm movements, starting from the rotating shoulder joint all the way to the multiple stages of angles produced by knuckles in your fingers. If you were to try to recreate all the movements of your hand with a robotic arm, you would need a moving component for every independent action of the arm. This means that the rotation of your wrist would be its own motor and gear assembly separate from the rotation of an elbow mechanism. Similarly, a factory welding robot needs mechanical control for every independent action or axis of articulation. Many of these robots need to be able to rotate at their base much like a shoulder. They need to be able to pivot and extend, like an elbow. Finally, they need to be able to rotate and make fine adjustments to get into position, like the joints in a wrist and hand.

Knowing these requirements for articulated movement, we can determine, without even beginning to design an arm, the number of motors or moving parts we might need to achieve such a range of actions. Even with one motor for every stage of articulation, the example we just mentioned would have at least four motors or actuators involved. Moreover, all of those motors would need to be sent power and signal through wires. You can already see how these simple facts about a system will get you thinking about ways to place motors such that you can still run wires to all of them in a frame. The length of sections in between each moving segment will ultimately be determined by the distance you need to be able to travel in each axis. For example, if the welding robot needs to reach parts of the car's frame that are well above the height of the arm at rest, you could assert that the elbow section must be long enough to pivot to such a height.

These questions about constraints and required actions are at the very foundation of the design process. Creativity truly shines when you can come up with as many answers as possible to a set of engineering problems. Brainstorming about the things that you can and cannot do with a robotic system will necessarily begin to generate ways to place components in a system. When paired with a mental toolbox that is filled with possible ways to connect moving parts, this method of inquiry is an incredibly effective generator of engineering solutions.

Finding Room on the Frame

When making plans for fitting together multiple systems in a robot, it's good to identify a couple of strategies to help you make decisions. Every robot is different, so every system will have a number of priorities or important factors to keep in mind as you start figuring out where to mount your parts. For instance, look at the kind of mechanisms and what they will require to operate. If you have a system of electrical motors and controllers, it can be wise to put the power source in a place that is easily accessible to run your wires without risk of entanglement. Alternatively, if you have a pneumatic mechanism, try to identify the best place for the compressor or air tank to make the most efficient configuration of hoses and valves.

Another critical thing to consider is the weight of components and their effects on a robot's **center of gravity**. Center of gravity is defined as an average of the position of weight on an object. Need to have a number of heavy batteries in the back of your robot? Try thinking of ways to put heavier components on the front end of the frame as a counterbalance to prevent the robot from tipping when moving. It's also good practice to avoid putting a large amount of weight on the top of a robotic system that moves around. The center of gravity should be as low as possible, or closest to the ground, to reduce the chance of gravity bringing a top-heavy robot straight to the ground. While these seem like the general concerns of physics, they can play a huge role in determining where certain parts of the robot go relative to their weight.

With those general concerns in mind, it's time to take a look at the physical limitations of your components. Moving systems need enough space to do their thing without grinding or wearing out over time. Proper tolerance of moving parts— the allowed amount of variation in their dimensions—can be

This robot was designed with a heavy armature in the center to promote balance while driving and operating.

critical not only to the safety of your parts, but also to their basic operation.

You can identify the possible range of motion of a mechanism by understanding its minimum and maximum positions. For instance, you could think of a rotating arm as having a starting position and an ending position based on how far it moves. The length of that arm will ultimately determine the amount of space it needs to move without obstruction or interference. In other words, if the moving segment of the arm is 3 feet (0.9 meters) long, then you could simply avoid placing objects within 3 feet of its starting position. This, of course, applies to the plane in which the arm is pivoting. For instance, you could easily place objects parallel to the movement of the arm without them getting in the way. However, it's when objects or frame components are at intersecting angles that they can begin to get in the way.

One way to more specifically calculate the tolerance for a rotating arm is by identifying the entire area of its cycle of movement. The volume of space, in three dimensions, that the mechanism can take up is determined ultimately by the kind of movement made and the size of the moving parts. So for a rotational movement, we can think of the area as a circle. For an example, you could consider an arm that can move an entire 360 degrees as occupying a space equal to the area of the circle produced by the length of the arm. If you were to use the formula for the area of the circle, the length of the arm would be the radius of that circle. Thus, $A = \pi r^2$ is the total area in which to avoid placing objects at intersecting angles or planes. For our 3-foot robot arm, this would mean $A = \pi 3^2$, or 9π, which is equal to 28.26 square feet (2.63 square meters) of area.

For mechanisms with linear movements, you can simply look at the dimensions of the mechanism at minimum and maximum extension. **Linear actuators**, for instance, extend a rod from an enclosed cylinder to a given limit based on the size of the cylinder. If you take the extended limits of the actuator and add any additional area from the attachments at the end of the rod, you can calculate the clearance necessary for the movement. For example, an actuator with a 1-foot (0.3 m) cylinder might have a rod that extends 10 inches (25 centimeters) when fully actuated. With a 4-inch (10 cm) claw attachment at the end of the rod, you have a maximum linear distance of 2.16 feet (12 inches + 10 inches + 4 inches = 26 inches, or 66 cm). Now it will be important to identify the width of the largest section of the actuator assembly. In this case, let's assume that the claw at the end is 6 inches (15 cm) wide when open and 2 inches (5 cm) tall. By multiplying all three dimensions—length, width, and height—you can calculate the volume that would be occupied by the movement of the fully open claw on the actuator. Thus, $26 \times 6 \times 2 = 312$ cubic inches (5,113 cubic centimeters) of volume. This volume designates a section of three-dimensional space that must be kept free of other components to allow the actuator to move freely. Anything within that volume could obstruct the motion of the actuator or provide resistance to the system.

This method can be used to get any tolerance of moving parts if you know the size of given components and the range of their motion. While certain linkages may not move in strictly linear or rotational fashion, you should be able to identify minimum and maximum values for a range of motion. Using this principle, any three-dimensional area can be calculated to get a required amount of space for a moving part or assembly. Using this information, you can begin to strategize placement of numerous mechanisms given their expected ranges of motion. However, just because two or more mechanisms may be in each other's potential range of motion, it doesn't mean they will necessarily run into each other. It can be good to identify cases where systems could *possibly* obstruct each other at full extension or specific positions, knowing that they won't be operational simultaneously. This is to say that ranges can overlap in instances where multiple systems don't need to function at the same time, allowing you to save space in your design for other functions.

DANGER: HOT SURFACE!

Mechanical and electrical components alike can get very hot under normal operation. In an electrical system, there are many components that expend excess energy as heat. An example of this is some types of voltage regulators that step down a given voltage to a lower voltage for a different component. The energy that is lost in the regulation process leaves the system as heat. In order to manage the resulting high temperatures, many components like this utilize machined pieces of thermally conductive material called **heatsinks**. Heatsinks dissipate heat across their surface

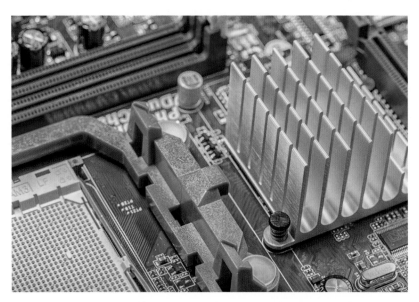

An aluminum heatsink with large air gaps between fins dissipates heat from a computer's motherboard.

area, which is then cooled by air passing over that surface. Heatsinks often have fins to maximize the airflow through the material. Aluminum is perhaps the most common heatsink material due to its thermally conductive properties and ability to be easily machined into thin fins.

The fact that some components can be putting off a hefty amount of excess heat should also inform your decisions for the placement of certain objects. For instance, it's a good idea to avoid putting small wires next to components that could get hot enough to deform or melt the wires' insulation. Additionally, components can sometimes get so hot that they fail to operate when they exceed their desired temperature range. This effect can be compounded when multiple heat sources are located in a confined area of a robot. As a result, you'll need to think of ways to position these parts next to places in the case that give them optimal airflow and cooling potential. One of the best ways to do this is by installing fans in the robot's frame. With one fan bringing airflow into the frame and another fan on the opposite side as an exhaust for hot air, you can keep temperatures of both electrical and mechanical components down to a manageable level.

Wire Management

One of the most critical steps in the design process is planning ample space to run wires. It is just as important that those wires are well protected from surrounding objects to avoid short circuits and risk of electrical fire. In this section, we will go over proper wire management and shielding techniques. Part of knowing how much space you will need to fit electrical components together is understanding what kinds of connectors you need as well as what size wire to use.

The size of a wire is ultimately determined by how much electrical current is going to be flowing through it. For instance, the wire you might use to power a drive motor on a robot will be fairly thick because of the amount of power drawn from the batteries. Alternatively, wires for sending communications or digital signals from sensors or controllers can be very thin due to the low amount of voltage and current being sent through the wire. The reason for this is that electrical current generates lots of heat on the copper strands of a wire. The larger the size of the wire, the more the current can be distributed, increasing the heat capacity. Trying to power heavy-duty motors with really thin wires runs the risk of burning up the conductor and melting through the protective insulation of the wire.

Some connections will require a decent amount of space to avoid putting stress on a connection or segment of wire. Wire is usually made of copper, which is a highly conductive material. Copper wire is often made up of finely braided strands, which make it flexible like rope or string. While this increases the wire's ability to move around, it is still very susceptible to kinks, which could cause the copper to break over time. Copper has a physical property called **work hardening**, which means that it becomes more brittle over time when placed under stress. If you take a piece of copper and bend it back and forth at a specific point, that point will quickly weaken until it breaks. This is important when considering the amount of stress placed on a wire over extended periods of use on a robot.

In order to avoid broken connections as a result of stress and work hardening, you must use proper **strain relief**. This is

Structural frame components are used to relieve strain on large wires in a system. Zip ties keep wires from getting tangled.

the displacement of the stress on a wire or connection achieved by securing the wire to a structural component. This means that the wire will be secured at a point away from the actual connection, allowing the terminal to be free of forces that may be acting on a wire. This is especially useful in cases where wires must move with mechanical components in order to stay connected. If a wire without proper strain relief gets pulled or yanked by a moving component, you run the risk of damaging the connection or even the component it's attached to.

Strain relief is an even greater concern with large-gauge wires because they are usually less flexible than small wires. In order to protect large wires that are rated for large amounts of current flow, the outer coating of the wire, or the insulation, must be quite thick. Wire insulation literally insulates the electrical connection from the outside of the wire, so it is important for this material to be strong, yet as flexible as possible. Silicone is a common insulation material as it allows for good wire movement but is easily punctured by sharp objects. Other insulation materials like thermoset can be much more rigid, thus requiring more space for bends and angles. Thermoset insulation is a plastic coating that is extruded onto a wire, then heated and pressurized. The resulting chemical process makes the insulation resistant to heat, preventing high electrical currents or external heat from melting the material. There are many different materials, each with its own set of pros and cons in terms of flexibility, durability, and resistance to heat. All three factors can be important in determining the space that will be occupied by wires in a robot.

Another way to protect wires is through bundling and/or shielding techniques. Even if wires are run together in a logical place out of harm's way, individual wires can be a hassle without wire management. Ever stick a pair of earbuds neatly in your pocket to find just a minute later that they're now a tangled mess? The same can happen to wires in a mechanical system, especially around other loose wires. One of the easiest solutions for this is to bind the wires together at regular intervals using durable string or **zip ties**. Zip ties, in particular, are widely used to get gangly wires under control due to their ease of use and locking nature.

Perhaps you'd also like to keep specific pairs or bundles of wires together. Without going through a whole bag of zip ties to achieve that result, you can clean up your wiring by twisting pairs or groups. For short lengths, this can be done easily by hand. For longer lengths, it's wise to take the wires you want

PROTECTING WIRES, SIGNALS

Putting braided metal shielding around groups of wires keeps wires together and safer from exposure to moving parts, especially if the wire is a small gauge. Electricity running through wires can be susceptible to **electromagnetic interference** (EMI) or radio frequency interference (RFI). This type of interference particularly affects communication signals through wires such as commands sent to a motor or data received by a sensor. Braided metal shields provide resistance to electromagnetic waves by surrounding the wires in a conductive material that affects the movement of the waves, ensuring good signal quality and avoiding interference.

to twist together and secure them to a table or vice. With one end secured, take the other end and clamp them together in the chuck of a hand drill. With the jaws of the drill tightly around the wires, you simply spin the tool in the direction you want them twisted. This technique makes quick work of longer wires and creates a nice, uniform twist. Twisted wires look very professional and can be very helpful when needing to run single pairs of wires out to a component.

There are many different types of connectors used to terminate the ends of wires. These connectors all have certain applications and can vary greatly in size, shape, and durability. Connectors, or **crimps**, used for large-gauge wires are often made to handle significant amounts of electrical current. In order to make a good high-current connection, larger crimps must have sufficient amounts of surface area to contact the conductor on both the wire and the component they're connected to. This means that the terminals can get rather bulky, requiring plenty of space to sit flat on the contact surface. Crimps are made of conductive materials like copper, brass, or tin, which are all metals that get brittle when bent. As a result, terminals should be given enough space to make a connection without needing to be bent or forced into place, or else the durability of the connection could be compromised.

Crimps and terminals can also be insulated like wires are. Insulation protects the ends of the connectors from making contact with unwanted surfaces or wires. This part is often a small plastic shield around the conductive material that gets pressed or crimped on a piece of wire. If terminals are non-insulated, however, it is always a good idea to provide a bit of insulation yourself. The quickest way to protect the ends of connectors is with **heatshrink**. This tube-like material can be fit over a wire or connection. Once the heatshrink is in the right place, you simply apply temperatures of about 200°F (93°C) or above, and the material shrinks until it holds tight around the connection. The material does stiffen the joint a bit, though, so be careful when planning for wires that need tight bends or loops.

Heatshrink is often an integral part of clean-cut wiring, and it makes connections safer and easier to work with. For instance, you will sometimes need to splice wires in order to power multiple devices from a single power source. Splicing wires involves the joining of conductive material, usually through a process called soldering. A soldered joint holds wires together by filling the spaces in between wire strands with a melted metal material called solder. The solder then hardens around the wires, forming a connection that is both structural and conductive. Without heatshrink, soldered connections would potentially be exposed to outside contact. While something like electrical tape can serve a similar function by covering exposed connectors, heatshrink has the advantage of never losing adhesion over time. Electrical tape can leave residue on the wire or even fall off if it is exposed to heat, so heatshrink is often the go-to for wiring needs.

Engineers also use a number of techniques to control wires that are attached to moving components. Let's say you were building a robot that needed to raise up to a 10-foot- (3 m) tall shelf, then grab and place objects all the way up there. Almost any way you slice it, in order to manipulate objects up that high, such a robot would need power and/or signal wires to reach up with whatever grabbing mechanism you made. This means that, for this kind of mechanism, you would need a bundle of wires at least 10 feet (3 meters) long to go up and down with the lifting components. Imagine for a second that you have all that wire extended to its limit. Even if it were bundled nicely, it would likely become tangled in some moving component or get wrapped up on itself when you brought the lift back down again.

So how do robot builders face such challenges? While there is no single answer to this type of question, the thinking behind a proper solution usually comes from a similar place. Whether by folding, rigging, or structural support, robot technicians overcome this challenge by controlling the manner in which the bundled wire moves in a way that is both expected and consistent. Only when you can ensure that a group of wires will move in a uniform fashion based on the movement of the mechanism it's attached to can you guarantee the reliable operation of such a system.

Let's look at a few examples of how to achieve this result. The first is a housing system called a **cable carrier**, or a drag chain. They are made up of sections joined by swiveling pins much like a tank **tread**. By putting a bundle of wires in the empty cavity inside the sections, the movement is limited to the direction that the segments can swivel. This makes it easier to establish a uniform movement and further protects the wires from outside harm. Cable carriers are very popular for industrial machines and robots because of this fact. In both electrical and

This robotic arm uses a cable carrier (light gray) to constrain and protect wires during movement.

pneumatic systems, cable carriers can reliably move wires or hoses directionally in instances of repetitive motion.

The next method is to use a coil or spring-like material to get repeated extension and compression of a cable. By running a group of wires through a coiled-up tube material, the connection is protected while gaining the spring-like properties of the housing. This can also drastically reduce the amount of space required to house long lengths of wire due to the efficient storage in the shape of a cylinder. Such a system has the advantage of returning to the same shape when the extension is complete. However, with heavy use, the springy qualities may wear out, depending on the material.

The last method is a bit more complex. You could actually have your wires wound up on a spool that unrolls as the lift extends. This system has perhaps the most predictable result given that the cables should spool out and spool back in the same orientation if executed properly. The complicated part of this system is the fact that it requires the electrical connection at the end of the spool to be able to spin. Unless your robot's battery is flipping end over end on the inside of a wire spool, you're going to need a different kind of connection to achieve this result. A device called a **slip ring** performs just such a task. Slip rings have a series of rotating brushes or commutators that make a connection to a conductive ring. This should sound very familiar from the discussion of brushed DC motors in chapter 1. The same kind of electrical connection is made to transfer current from a stationary conductor to one that rotates. Slip rings are very common in any winch-like operation such as this where you need power at the end of a tether or spool.

Limiting Robotic Movements

Spacing between robotic components can already be tight in a moving system. Think about a scenario in which you have a moving part that could possibly collide with the robot's frame or even other components if it moves too far. This is commonly the case anywhere you have a motor for a **lever** or claw. Due to the fact that the motor has the ability to spin 360 degrees and beyond, it's easy to see how moving the motor too far could cause a problem when the arm of a claw rotates beyond its intended range. Robot builders have to constantly be thinking about the potential ranges of their mechanisms when fitting components together, and a huge part of that is finding ways to limit the movement of various pieces.

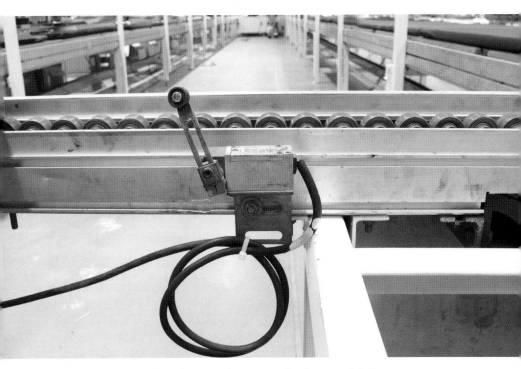

A limit switch is used to trigger actions on a robotic assembly line.

Limiting motion can be done with both programming and hardware solutions. Oftentimes both methods are necessary to give enough control to a system. One of the most common examples of this kind of hybrid solution is a **limit switch**. A limit switch is effectively a button that sends a signal to a microcontroller or relay when pressed. Instead of being a button that the user presses on the robot, limit switches are triggered by the movement of mechanical components. More generally, they are known as touch sensors and give robots the ability to sense if a moving part has hit a limit or obstacle. For a rotating lever like the arm of a claw, it's a good idea to put limit switches on a part of the arm that could come into contact with a piece, which then presses the button. As a result, the limit switch requires a hardware counterpart to press the switch that is placed at the desired physical boundary of the mechanism. This hardware piece is often a part of a robot's frame, making for easy identification of boundaries for the mechanism.

Motion can also be limited on a purely mechanical basis. If you need a lever to rotate to a maximum of 60 degrees, you can rather easily put a piece of aluminum tube right at that degree marker to stop the motion and cause the motor to stall. Such a configuration is called a mechanical stop and physically prevents motion beyond a structural component. These stops can be rough on motors or frame components if the force exerted on the mechanical stop is large. As a result, it's often best to implement a combination of mechanical stops and software solutions. Mechanical stops have the advantage of peace of mind if a bit of software bugs out or is in need of calibration.

As hinted above, another solution would be a purely programmed approach. This approach will require sufficient sensors for a given mechanism so you have **feedback** for a controller to work with. If the arm needs to reach exactly 60 degrees, how will the controller know how far it's traveled? For this example, you could use a motor encoder as a sensor attached to the shaft of the motor. The encoder will give you feedback on how far, in degrees, the arm moves, allowing you to identify 60 degrees as a value to stop the motor. It is usually a good idea to smooth the movement of the motor by slowing it down as it approaches your desired value. For instance, if you wanted 60 degrees, you could start slowly decelerating at around 45 degrees. This will help prevent your motor from overshooting if it is moving with too much inertia when the command to stop the motor is issued by the microcontroller.

Conclusion

When you look at the inside of a robot, it can sometimes be hard to imagine how the engineers and technicians got it all to fit in there. In this chapter, we looked at a few strategies for designing with space and function in mind. With every moving component comes a volume of space that it needs to occupy. Calculating space requirements can be a good first step for planning the placement of systems in a robot. Additionally, good robot design always has wiring and cable management in mind from the outset of a project. Knowing full well that all of your moving systems will need power of one sort or another, planning ahead on how to distribute that power is an integral part to a good robot build. Clean wiring practices not only make systems easy on the eyes, they make robots safer for both operation and maintenance when all conductors are properly insulated and secured. Lastly, it is important to place limitations on moving components using both physical and software solutions. Preventing motors or actuators from extending beyond a desired range with devices like limit switches can be critical for the operation of robotic mechanisms. By bracketing off ranges of motion with your designs and programming strategies, you can begin to fit the pieces together safely and efficiently.

Robotic gantries efficiently lift entire cars with mechanical advantage.

3 Basic Machines and Power Systems

In physics, the term "work" refers to the product of force on an object and how much an object is moved by that force. By their very nature, robots do work to perform tasks or achieve certain goals. A robot that stands on two legs and walks does work by moving the weight of its body over a given distance per step. Robots in an industrial factory do work when they lift heavy objects from one place to another, or when they repeatedly produce manufactured objects and send them down a conveyor belt. In the everyday sense of the word, robots also perform lots of work and help us complete tasks that are beyond our working ability as humans. They have the advantage of working with extreme degrees of precision, with incredible amounts of force, and with the ability to produce consistent results from repeated motion. The work done by robots is often highly efficient compared to the abilities of humans given a similar task. While some jobs or products absolutely require the finesse and judgment of human hands, robotic systems shine in applications in which large-scale production is required.

In order to do their work, robots use powered mechanisms that are connected to move into various positions with a given amount of force. In this chapter, we'll go over which mechanisms will be right for the job based on a number of criteria. Looking at the advantages and disadvantages of parts in individual systems, we will show that there are large numbers of ways to solve nearly every engineering problem given the right set of tools. By asking the question "What work needs to be done?" we can begin to narrow the kinds of mechanisms that are able to tackle certain tasks. This chapter will be divided into sections based on a couple of common ways that robots do work for us. Whether it's transportation, heavy lifting, or calculated small movement, there's a set of mechanisms that have been proven to work in all everyday applications.

Basic Machines

You are probably familiar with the six simple machines from a past science class. While the classic examples of each simple machine see lots of use in everyday life, it's good to look at the ways that they fit into more complex arrangements. The six simple machines were postulated during the Renaissance as the fundamental basis of every moving part or machine. Time periods since the Industrial Revolution have produced great numbers of mechanical parts and connectors that can be used to make compound mechanisms. As a result, we can identify all constituent parts of robots and robotic systems as basic machines. In this section, we will go over a number of basic machines and their practical usage in robotic applications.

From that point, we can jump into a number of compound assemblies and explain how they work in terms of their basic machine components.

The first basic machine is an **inclined plane**. The inclined plane is a tilted material or surface that uses the potential energy from gravity to move objects. In its most simple form, an inclined plane is a kind of ramp for spherical objects to roll down. A pinball machine operates on this kind of basic structure, using the gravitational pull on the ball toward the bottom of the machine to ensure the ball's return from various other moving parts of the system. The principle of the inclined plane can be applied to all sorts of linkages that include systems with slides or tracks. These basic machines have been very powerful for engineering applications from the construction of the Great Pyramids to wheelchair-accessible ramps.

Very close to the inclined plane is the **wedge**. The wedge is a triangular object used for the separation of objects or parts from an object, lifting, or holding an object stationary. When force is applied directionally to a wedge from the blunt end opposite the smallest angle of the triangle, the force spreads an object or objects across the inclined surfaces of the wedge. As a basic machine, wedges give mechanical advantage over an object as a ratio of its width and the length of the inclined surface. Wedges are a good basis for lifting mechanisms because of the way they can separate an object from the surface of a floor. Think of the front of a forklift, which has inclined surfaces at the ends of the prongs. By driving the forklift with the prongs against the ground, the wedges can get under heavy objects for the forklift to manipulate. Also important to the world of robotics and manufacturing, blades are a kind of wedge that separate pieces or chips from material. Cutting tools can be the intersection of two or three inclined planes at an edge or point. When force is applied to this edge against a material, the cutting tool overcomes the resistance of the material and pushes pieces to either side of the tool face. In most cases, the amount removed by each cutting pass is only a few thousandths of an inch at a time for machining operations.

While you might be familiar with screws as a fastener for materials like wood or metal, screws are also basic machines. Using a series of threads against a surface that is threaded translates rotational motion and torque into linear motion. One of the more common examples of this basic machine is called a **lead screw**. Imagine you have a nut threaded onto a long screw or piece of threaded rod. If the rotational motion of the nut is constrained or fixed to a track such that it does not spin with the screw, then the nut will move in a linear direction based on the direction of the screw's rotation. Lead screws are used widely in robotics applications where you need precise linear movement using a motor as the source of the rotational force. Robotic manufacturing equipment or CNC machines often use lead screws to feed a cutting or shaping tool into a piece of raw material.

Screws are also not limited to applications where they have a threaded counterpart as a mechanical system. They can also be used to move materials in a linear fashion when surrounded by a tube or channel. These systems are called conveyor screws, or Archimedes screws, and use wider helical or spiral blades as their threads. Objects become confined between threads

The first use for an Archimedes screw such as this one was collecting water against the flow of gravity.

and the force of gravity keeps them against the front face of the helical blade. This makes it so the objects travel toward the top of the rotating screw by riding the thread the whole way up. The Archimedes screw was conceived as a system for water collection and transportation from a source. Since then, engineers have used conveyor screws called augers as a way of drilling or for the transportation of mass-produced objects in a manufacturing plant.

The **wheel and axle** is a basic machine that is integral to every robotic system in some shape or form. As the very basis upon which motors are implemented in mechanical applications, the wheel and axle translates rotational force from an axle to the wheel or vice versa. You can think of a winch device with a hand crank as a wheel and axle that translates rotation starting from the wheel. Alternatively, a motor shaft attached to a gear provides force that can be changed according to the diameter of the gear. The ratio of the radius of the shaft or axle to the radius of the wheel determines the mechanical advantage of this basic machine. Wheel and axle assemblies are very often paired with bearings, which allow for the free spinning rotation of the axle in place. Ball bearings are comprised of a series of small spheres that line a track on the inside of a ring. The spheres spin as they move around the track, causing the inner circle of the ring that holds a shaft to rotate. Bearings are used to reduce the friction between an axle and a mounting surface. For instance, if a shaft were mounted in the same sized hole in a piece of material instead of being mounted in a bearing, the friction would prohibit smooth (if any) movement of the shaft.

Similar in many ways to the wheel and axle, pulleys are another basic machine used in all fields of engineering, including robotics. Effectively, pulleys take the concept of a wheel and axle and use the surface of the circumference of either component to provide mechanical advantage. For instance, a rope wrapped around a wheel at the end of an axle will rotate around the circumference of the wheel, which allows the directional change of the force on the rope. Imagine a large mechanism like a crane used to move steel beams on a construction site. The cables used to lift the heavy beams pick the material up perpendicular to the ground, but the cable runs the length of the crane's arm at a given angle. This allows the crane's mechanical winch to lift the beams with rotational force by changing the direction of the force with the pulley at the top of the crane.

In robotics, one of the most common implementations of pulleys is for belt systems. Flat belts ride along the circumference of pulleys that are attached to axles or shafts. These belts allow for the translation of rotational force across the distance of the belt between two wheels. Robots very often make use of belt pulley systems to use a single motor to control multiple systems.

TIP ON WHEELS AND PULLEYS

The size of the wheels or pulleys will determine the different rotational rates of the connected shafts and systems, meaning that you can get different speeds from a single rotational source.

A lever is a very important basic machine for robotics. A lever is defined as a rigid section of material that pivots at a point of rotation called a fulcrum. Levers are the basis of every robotic armature, and their use can provide a mechanical advantage to lift heavy objects. The fulcrum for robotic or mechanical levers is usually a rotating joint from a motor or wheel and axle assembly. Levers are also common as parts of larger assemblies because they can connect multiple moving systems with rigid beams. When you think about it, a lever can also be used to create an inclined plane when the angle of the material changes over the fulcrum. This means that the pivot from the fulcrum can allow objects to be guided down the slope of the lever when it is engaged or disengaged. For this reason, levers are used frequently in robots to act like gates that open and close to control objects.

Robots can utilize this kind of lever assembly in manufacturing applications to move production pieces from one part of a system to another in a calculated manner. For instance, an industrial assembly line will frequently measure out specific numbers of pieces to be packaged and will use levers like gates to regulate the amount. These systems are often based on functions of time that are related to other parts of the automated system. An assembly line could use the amount of time it takes to produce a certain number of pieces, then open the gate at a regular time interval based on the size of the package. Some robotic systems that manufacture lots of small pieces use time to determine the amount of material that will flow, due to gravity, from the gate mechanism when it opens. Boxes of cereal are sometimes filled this way using calculated moments of opening and closing robotic gates or valves.

Kinematics and Camshafts

We have just taken a look at the six fundamental machines. These can be very useful when looking at a system to identify how it works. All of these basic machines fall under a more specific branch of mechanics called **kinematics**. The term kinematics refers to a field of classical mechanics that describes the relative movement of objects in a system without considering the mass of those objects or the forces responsible for their movement. Kinematics, as a field, helps us to understand how bodies move together based on their linkages or constraints. Two bodies that move together with imposed constraints are known as a kinematic pair. Think of two gears with their teeth enmeshed. When one gear rotates, the second gear will rotate in the opposite direction as part of its constrained movement as a kinematic pair.

FORCEFUL WORDS

The term "kinematic pair" was coined by mechanical engineer Franz Reuleaux in the 1800s. Reuleaux was considered the Father of Kinematics for his contributions to the field of academic engineering.

It can be helpful to think about the motion of mechanical pieces through the lens of kinematics. This means that all mechanisms and assemblies can be viewed as a set of constraints based on the linkages between solid pieces. In other words, a lever is bound to a certain kind of movement based on the linkage provided by the fulcrum. The length of the solid material is there to connect to other linkages that will drive further motion as part of an assembly. Complex sets of moving parts can be explained more clearly by looking at the kinds of linkages connecting sections of pieces in motion. Using this model of understanding, we can look at a good example of a mechanism with multiple linkages that changes motion from rotational to linear.

A camshaft uses the compression of pistons to create powerful rotation in an axle.

A **cam** is a mechanism that uses rotating or sliding pieces to transfer rotational motion into linear motion and vice versa. One of the most common examples is a wheel of a steam engine train. Ever notice the long bar that moves linearly with the rotation of the wheel? This is a cam that uses a spinning linkage on the outside of the wheel to rotate in a back-and-forth linear motion. The linear motion is provided by a piston that moves when pressure from steam builds up in the cylinder behind it. That pressure moves the cam and the rotating linkage on the wheel constrains it to a pedaling-like motion.

A combustion engine in almost every car also uses a series of cams in a similar way to produce rotation in the wheels. A number of cams connected to a central rotating linkage is called a camshaft. The camshaft rotates when the pistons are moved in their cylinders from the pressure of fuel combustion. The small combustion in every cylinder pushes the pistons up and drives the camshaft at a particular part of its rotation. Individual cams in a camshaft are offset so that there's force being applied to the rotation of the drive shaft at every phase of the rotation.

What would happen if you constrained the movement of the bottom of the cam with another linkage? If the end of the cam is attached with another pivot to an object that fits into a channel or chamber, you can produce linear actuation. This type of cam is called a piston and uses the physical constraints of the chamber around the piston to direct the motion of the cam that is attached by rotating linkages. Combustion engines in cars work by using a series of pistons to move a camshaft to produce the rotation of the axle. The force of combustion pushes the pistons at different phases of the shaft's rotation, creating a smooth and continuous movement for the axle.

Camshafts also don't have to be directly linked to the linear actuators they move. If you have a wheel with the pivot point not centered so one side is slightly skewed out, it will cause an irregular rotational pattern. Every time this irregular section passes over a linear actuator, the additional length of that section will press down on the piston mechanism.

These irregular wheels are called eccentric discs and are made specifically to create motion for actuators at specific intervals based on the speed of the camshaft's rotation.

Belts and Chains

Belts and chains are used to connect two or more wheel and axle assemblies. Both rely on a certain amount of tension to transfer motion between wheels or gears and sprockets. One of the wheel and axle assemblies drives the other via the friction of a belt or the mechanical pull of a chain. While they serve very similar functions, belts and chains often have their own specific applications based on a number of advantages and disadvantages of each.

Belts are usually a single piece of circular material which is manufactured to be a particular size to fit a spacing between two wheels. Belts can be made from strips of material when they are sewn or melted together, but the junction will usually cause a slight bump when it runs over the wheels. Belts come in a number of different materials like rubber, cloth, and composites like Kevlar. The material is determined by the amount of desired elasticity of the belt as well as structural integrity and surface friction. More elastic materials like rubber can provide good tension between wheels but will eventually snap from extended use. As a result, many belts in automobiles are lined with materials like Kevlar, which is a stranded material found in bulletproof vests. This limits the stretching capabilities of a belt but increases its resistance to damage over time.

Perhaps the most important feature of belts is that they can be made to fit the width of nearly any wheel. Wide, flat

A timing belt is used on a pulley to increase precision and prevent slippage.

belts are known as conveyor belts and can be used to transport materials on a robotic system. In nearly every grocery store, the checkout counter will have a section of conveyor belt to move products to be scanned. Robots use this same style of mechanism for complex manufacturing operations or object manipulation. Conveyor belts are usually slower in operation and require a bit more torque from the motors to move so much surface area.

There are also special belts called **timing belts,** which are paired with certain kinds of gears. These timing belt gears have indentations that correspond to bumps or teeth in the timing belt. These teeth prevent the belt from slipping and ensure the position of the belt relative to the rotation of the gear. They are called timing belts because the teeth give a numerical value to the distance the belt travels with every rotation. These belts operate consistently and quietly, making them good for belt-driven mechanisms for household use.

Chains are most similar to timing belts in that they correspond to the intervals of teeth on a gear or sprocket. Chains are first and foremost different from belts because they are modular, meaning they consist of sections that can be put together. The size of a chain is determined by the amount of links you put in before you close it with a master link. A master link is the part of a chain with a removable clip that allows you to add or take out links without destroying the chain. This is especially handy if the position of sprockets changes over the course of the project, necessitating a different length of chain. In addition, you can change the tension of a chain by removing a link and closing small gaps. While the most common chains are made of steel, they still wear and stretch slightly over time, meaning you could have to remove a link to retain the desired amount of tension between two wheels.

Each segment of a chain is itself a rotational linkage. In order to prevent wear on these linkages, chains need to be greased or lubricated. Ever accidently reached down and touched the chain on your bicycle and gotten your hands all gunked up? That's because the chain was submerged in an oil bath when it was manufactured to keep the linkages free of dirt and moving smoothly. The segments of a chain are spaced specifically to match up to the spacing of teeth on a sprocket. A sprocket is a special kind of wheel with teeth at regular intervals that mesh with the empty space between linkages on a chain. If properly tensioned, chains rarely skip because of the close hold they have on the teeth of a sprocket, making the transfer of motion very efficient between two axles.

Unlike belts, chains are not often used to transfer objects or materials on their surface due to their relative width. However, it is possible to attach additional linkages to the outside of a chain. Robotic systems sometimes use parallel sections of chains as mounting points for baskets or collectors. This allows you to turn a vertical section of chains and sprockets into a sort of elevator assembly in which materials ride up as the motor drives the chain around. This kind of system is useful in applications like harvesting and mining due to the repeated gathering of materials from a ground location.

Drive Systems

Outside of the world of industry and manufacturing, robots often need to move around and travel great distances. Some robots gather up dust from the floor in your home, while some gather up dust on the surface of Mars, by getting around on drive systems. Drive systems use the rotation of motors with wheel and axle assemblies in a number of different ways. The tiny robot vacuum cleaner in your house is built with very tiny wheels close to the surface of the floor so it can effectively clean. The rovers on Mars are built with very large wheels and complex suspension systems to face the challenges presented by martian terrain. Drive systems are engineered to fit the task of moving around in the environment that is expected of a given robot. In this section, we will go over a few common aspects of drive systems and take a look at their relevant applications.

Let's start with the most straightforward drive system: wheels. Wheels help you get around in everyday life in mechanical applications like automobiles and bicycles. Ever wonder why their usage is so widespread as opposed to different kinds of drive systems? First and foremost, wheels are good for applications where speed is desirable due to the relatively low amount of torque required to move them from a rest point. They are also cheap and easy to manufacture, making them accessible for any robot builder. Depending on how the wheels are hooked up to a number of motors, wheels can give incredible control and maneuverability.

The size of the wheels also plays a big role in their capabilities for certain applications. The larger the wheel, the greater the surface area that will make contact with the driving

MATH MOMENT

If a wheel is connected directly to the output shaft on a motor, every rotation will move the robot equal to the measurement of the wheel's circumference in distance. Let's see what this actually means in terms of two different-sized wheels. Say you have two wheels that are 3 inches (7.6 cm) in diameter and 5 inches (12.7 cm) in diameter, respectively. Given the formula $C = 2\pi r$ for the circumference of a circle, we can calculate the distance each wheel would travel in a single rotation. For the first wheel, we would set up the equation $2 \times 3.14 \times 1.5 = 9.42$ inches (23.9 cm). The second wheel would be $2 \times 3.14 \times 2.5 = 15.7$ inches (39.9 cm) traveled in a single rotation. As a result, the 5-inch wheel would travel more than 6 inches (16 cm) farther per rotation of the motor than the 3-inch wheel. Depending on the revolutions per minute (rpm) of the motor, that difference in distance traveled could quickly add up to a big difference in speed.

An omni wheel gives a robot the ability to move in any direction using a series of exterior rollers.

surface. This means that the traction will increase with wheels that are larger in both width and diameter. The diameter of the wheel also determines the distance the robot will travel for every rotation of a drive motor. However, the larger the wheel, the more force will need to be applied to overcome inertia.

Wheels can also be controlled in a number of complex and interesting ways. Lunar and martian rovers move around their environments with ease due to their agile suspension systems. Each axle of a robot like this has linear actuators that control and smooth the angle of the wheels as they move over uneven terrain. This allows for the rovers to get over small obstacles without getting stuck and ensures that all the wheels are touching the surface at all times to retain traction. These rovers operate solely on solar power, so every bit of movement needs to be efficient and calculated toward certain goals.

There are also variations on the wheel that are called **omni wheels**. These innovative parts are comprised of a number of rollers, which surround the circumference of the wheel. The rollers can be set up to spin either perpendicular to or adjacent to the rotation of the entire wheel. This allows the wheel to move from side to side instead of creating friction when force is applied in a heading other than its primary driving direction.

Some omni wheels are configured such that all four wheels are driven separately. When two motors on opposite sides of the robot drive in opposing directions, the omni wheels rotate on their rollers, which causes the robot to move in the direction of the rollers. This means that a robot can actually drive *sideways* and move around like a crab on the floor. This drive system is incredibly useful for applications where the robot needs to be positioned facing a goal or for tracking an object in a certain direction. Imagine moving in any direction you want without ever having to turn!

Treads or continuous track systems are also commonly used for robotic applications. Treads are a bit more specialized than wheels due to certain characteristics, and as such, they are not always necessary in cases where wheels are sufficient. These assemblies are made up of a number of wheels connected by a segmented track that rotates against the outer surface of the wheels. As a result, tread systems have a large amount of surface area in constant contact with the ground, making for large amounts of traction. This surface area also more evenly distributes the weight of the robot on the driving surface, making it more ideal for massive industrial machines that need to move hundreds of tons of material.

Since the wheels in a continuous track system are all connected by the tread, they all must move at the same time in the same direction. This requires a much greater amount of torque to overcome the inertia of the mechanism. Tread systems thus require a greater amount of power and are less efficient than wheels in normal driving conditions. However, in situations where traction is needed to scale obstacles or handle

A robot with treads traverses a grassy environment without spinning in place, thereby delivering a ball in time for kickoff.

smoothly on shifting terrain, treads can end up being more efficient by avoiding spinouts.

On the negative side, the treads themselves can break under stress, rendering the entire drive system useless. Once

DEAN KAMEN'S LUKE ARM

Dean Kamen is an inventor who has received hundreds of patents over his career. He uses engineering as an opportunity to help change the world in positive ways by making life easier for people who need it. His engineering company, DEKA, has been working on a robotic arm for amputees and combat veterans called the "Luke Arm." Kamen got the name from a Star Wars movie when the hero, Luke Skywalker, gets his hand chopped off and then replaced with a fully functional bionic hand. Using sensors that pick up electrical signals from the muscles of an amputee,

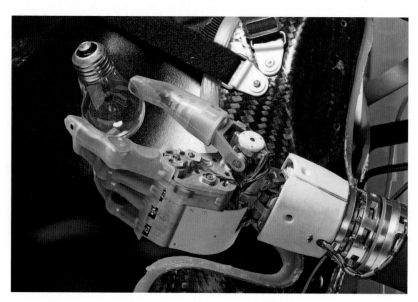

The hand on a Luke Arm holds a fragile lightbulb without dropping or shattering it.

the Luke Arm controls motors which account for up to ten different points of motion. Just like a normal human arm, this robotic invention can rotate and move in multiple axes at the same time. This means the user can reach down and open his or her hand to pick up an object with fluidity and accuracy. This allows patients to perform everyday tasks like opening doors with keys or even preparing food.

The hand of the Luke Arm is particularly astonishing in its precision. Pressure sensors give feedback to the wearer; they let the wearer know how much to close the hand around delicate objects. The hand is so good at this that a wearer can hold a grape without crushing or dropping it as it reaches his or her mouth. This is impressive due to the small but powerful motors that need to fit inside the size of a normal hand. Imagine that every possible movement your hand could make would be replaced by a motor or mechanical assembly. Add up all the wiring and sensors and you've got an incredible amount of technology in a very tight space. Part of the wonder of the Luke Arm is the fact that it was made not only to be equivalent to the size of a human arm, but also to its weight.

they break they can be expensive and difficult to repair. Additionally, the track material wears down more quickly than a normal tire due to the amount of movement it undergoes under tense conditions. Vehicles with treads also take a very long time to turn as the treads are limited to forward and reverse. With two sets of treads, you can only spin them in opposite directions to turn. This style of steering is called **tank drive** for this very reason.

Power Systems

With all these moving parts in your robot, you're going to need a way to power them. While most industrial robots get their power from high voltage outlets in a factory, the robots that move around have to have a more portable power source. Batteries come in a range of sizes, voltages, and capabilities. Much of this variation comes from the type of material that makes up the electrochemical cells that store a battery's charge. You may be familiar with commercial batteries that power your small electronics at home. These kinds of batteries are generally single-use, or **primary batteries**, meaning they cannot be recharged. The reason for this is that the electrochemical materials in the batteries are irreversibly altered when they are discharged to power a device. Secondary batteries, on the other hand, are rechargeable, meaning the cells can restore voltage if a reverse current is applied from a charger. Any battery in your phone or MP3 player is a secondary battery and charges when you give it electrical current from an adapter on a wall outlet.

Robots are also generally powered with secondary batteries so they can run again and again after a bit of time on the charger.

The most common kind of secondary battery is a lead acid battery. These batteries are relatively inexpensive for their capacity and can output large amounts of power. Due to the fact that they have lead in their very name, these batteries are incredibly heavy and often very large. They are most commonly used as automobile batteries because of how easily they can be recharged whenever the car starts up. For robotic applications, small lead acid batteries can be great due to their power output if weight is not a large concern. They can generally withstand more than two hundred cycles of full charge and recharge, making them ideal for regular operation.

Nickel metal hydride batteries, or "NiMh" batteries, are a common choice for small robots. They are easily rechargeable with little memory effect, meaning that they charge to the same full capacity every time. These kinds of batteries are desirable because of their average of price, capacity, and weight. They usually come in compact little bricks of cylindrical cells and can be fit into almost any robot frame of around 1 cubic foot (0.03 cubic meters).

Lithium ion batteries are also found in lots of consumer electronics. In most cases, the rechargeable battery in your phone is lithium ion as they can be very small and last for long durations. Laptops also use this kind of battery due to its ability to effectively charge while in the device it's powering. Lithium ion batteries are rectangular due to the chemical construction of the cells inside the battery, making them good for small, flat

This commercial drone is flying on power provided by a light but powerful lithium polymer battery.

electronic devices. More recently, lithium ion batteries have been used to power electric cars due to their efficiency and life over long periods of time. The Tesla Model S uses a lithium ion battery with more than seven thousand individual cells! The design of this battery allows for enough recharge cycles so that the car can travel up to 125,000 miles (201,200 kilometers) before needing to swap out the battery.

Lithium polymer batteries have the greatest ratio of weight to power and pack an enormous electrical capacity. These batteries are also rather expensive but are necessary for certain applications. Drones and other flying robots use **LiPo batteries** to have enough power to get thrust from the motors without weighing the craft down with excess weight. While flight time for a single LiPo battery on a drone can be as little as a few minutes, this kind of battery has made drone technology possible due to the high rate of discharge for generating lift. The voltage of a LiPo battery increases with the number of cells at increments of 3.7 volts. A six-cell LiPo battery is common for powering drones because many high-power hobby motors are made to run at around 24 volts ($3.7 \times 6 = 22.2$ V).

Calculating Battery Life

Once you've decided on the kind of battery material that's best for your application, you can begin to look at the power requirements for your system. Batteries have a specified voltage that decreases as the charge gets distributed to electronic and mechanical systems. The rate of discharge is determined by the power consumption of devices on your robot. The battery's capacity is expressed in terms of current over time, known as milliamp hours. A milliamp is a measurement of electrical current, or the rate of energy flow from the battery's terminals. As such, the milliamp hour measures the amount of energy transferred at a steady rate of one milliamp for the duration of an hour.

Batteries also have another relevant value called a **C-rate**. The C-rate is a measurement of how long it takes the battery to discharge based on its capacity and current flow. The measurement of 1C means that a battery will discharge its

An array of batteries are wired in parallel for increased capacity.

entire capacity over the span of a single hour. If a battery has a rating of 3,500 mAh—mAh is an abbreviation for milliamp hour—with a C-rate of 2C, it will discharge 3,500 mA in just thirty minutes. If it has a C-rate of 0.5, it will discharge 3,500 mA in two hours, or 1,750 mA per hour.

Here is another example: If a battery has a 6,000 mAh rating with a C-rate of 1C, it can discharge 6,000 milliamps over the course of an hour. If a robot is using a steady current of 1,000 milliamps, how long would the battery last? If you divide the capacity by the rate of current flow on the robot, you would get (6,000/1,000 = 6). This means that you would get a six-hour battery life using that amount of current draw.

Let's look at a more realistic example by adding up the current draw of a few systems for a robot. Take, for example, a 12-volt DC motor that has a maximum current draw of 10 amperes (1 ampere = 1,000 milliamps). If your robot's drivetrain has two of these motors, then how large of a battery would you need to be able to run them at full speed for five minutes? While it's not usually the case that a robot will need to operate at such a high level for so long, it's a good test to see what the *smallest* capacity you could get away with using would be.

With a few units to work with, we can start crunching the numbers. Taking the above example, 10 amps = 10,000 milliamps of current (10 × 1,000 mA). With two motors, we would draw 20,000 milliamps of current. Since we're only trying to operate these motors for a fraction of an hour, let's divide the number of milliamps by the same fraction to get our current draw over time. Five minutes is equal to one-twelfth of an hour. As such, we divide 20,000 by 12 and get approximately 1,667 mA. This value represents the amount of milliamps of current drawn by the motors over a period of five minutes.

With those values in mind, you actually have a range of options for your battery. Since the mAh rating and the C-rate are both significant to the discharge rate, you can find a few different configurations that would fit the requirements of this robotic experiment. For instance, if you had a 1,667 mAh battery, what C-rate would you need to discharge it over the course of five minutes? You would again divide an hour (60/5) to get a C-rate of 12. Batteries with high C-rates are less common because they are used in specific applications where you need high power over a short amount of time. Flying vehicles like drones rely on batteries with C-rates upwards of 50C! If you wanted to find a battery with a smaller C-rate of around 3C, you could simply multiply the milliamp hour rate by the amount you divided the C-rate. Since we divided the C-rate by 4, we can multiply the milliamp hour rate by the same value to get 6,668 mAh. As you can see, there are many configurations that would work to fit this need based on the C-rate and mAh rating, respectively. For this application, you could safely go with a 7,000 mAh battery with a C-rate of 3C.

Conclusion

In this chapter, we covered a large range of mechanisms and their relevant applications in robotics. By now you should be getting a good picture of how basic elements can play integral roles in complicated assemblies. Even the most sophisticated robots like martian rovers and robotic arms are based around elementary principles of basic machines and kinematics. An understanding of how various linkages work will necessarily increase your understanding of mechanical systems at large and the orchestration of moving parts.

From here, we can begin to dive a bit more into the practical realm of how robots are built and the challenges you can face when designing and putting them together. In the next chapter, we will go over a number of problem-solving techniques and strategies, taking a special look at times in the real world when engineers have had to band together to overcome obstacles in robotics. Just as the moving pieces in an assembly need to work together to achieve goals and perform tasks, so too do the teams of people that make robots a reality in everyday life.

A rugged, self-driving robot rolls through a rocky environment to make a delivery to a home.

4 Problem Solving with Robotics

Problem solving is an integral part of the process of building robots. This is twofold in that engineers and technicians use robots to solve complex and challenging problems in the world around them and beyond. In addition to the challenges of solving a problem with mechanical means, these engineers also have to face a significant amount of troubleshooting and problem solving to get things working together. This can also mean figuring out how to effectively work together as a team to complete tasks that are too great for any single individual.

In this chapter, we will look at a number of problem-solving strategies in robotics and how they apply to various stages of the building process. In the design phase, engineers must think creatively to find out how mechanical automation can be used to better suit the needs of a community or profession. This includes considerations like the role of human interface with the machines as well as quality and safety of operations. An important part of designing and building robots is giving proper consideration to a range of ideas and engineering philosophies from an entire group. Learning how to balance ideas and work together as a team is critical to the success of any large robotics project. Even when the robot is nearly completed, problem-solving strategies will be needed to address how it functions in a real-world scenario. This process of troubleshooting and **debugging** takes the robotics project out of the world of design and simulation and into an environment where real factors determine the kinds of changes that need to be made to turn a mere prototype into a hard-working robot.

Robotic Solutions

Robots address a huge range of problems in our world. Whether it's for efficiency in the manufacturing world or for mechanical processes that help people to live easier and safer lives, robots can be used as answers for very difficult questions. As such, the first part of any venture into robotics is looking at the kinds of questions you want to answer in the world. How can we better recycle plastics? How could we provide safe drinking water for small communities all over the world? How could I more easily vacuum my floor at home? From the global to the local and the personal, robotics can be a way to think about problems. There are certainly answers to these kinds of questions that are social, political, and economic. Robotics gives you an opportunity to address certain concerns mechanically, often by coming up with new and inventive ways to tackle an issue.

With a good question in mind that you'd like to solve with robotics, you can get a bit more specific to determine a number of constraints for the project. How big does it have to be to achieve its goals? What is the budget or price range for your project, and what kinds of parts are available to you? How long will it be designed to operate and under what kinds of conditions? All of these questions are part of the first steps in designing a robot. The more you know about the problem, the more effectively you can begin to think of solutions in terms of moving parts.

Whenever NASA sends a rover to Mars or to the moon, it looks at the challenges posed by the environment, the capabilities for communications across immense distances, and the kinds of samples and data they need to capture, among many other concerns. Before a wheel or gear is ever conceived or designed, the rovers are defined by their mission. You can think of any project in robotics with a mission in mind. Whether the mission is to autonomously drive your trash can

This 3-D rendering shows the Mars Rover in its working environment.

to the curb or to collect samples of soil on the surface of Mars, your mission will determine the way you begin to think about mechanical solutions.

Let's take the example of something mundane like building a robot to take out the trash every week. What kind of driveway or path do you have where you live? If it's a driveway, then a simple drivetrain with four wheels might be a logical place to start for the movement of the robot. Is it dirt or grass? Try to consider larger wheels with inflatable tires to get over any bumps in the terrain with ease. Is the path covered in rocks or roots that pose more serious challenges? Look into treads for their traction and ability to scale inclines. This is a great starting place for thinking about the ways in which the conditions of a mission will affect the design process. Notice that without even considering the configuration of the drivetrain, we can still make informed decisions about the kinds of parts you'll need to do the task.

Moving a bit further into the technical aspects of the problem, let's look at the objects your robot is carrying. Assuming for a second that the trash can can start on the robot, how will it be secured to the moving robot? Will this involve some kind of claw or lever for a gate? Keep in mind that this mechanism should also serve a function in dropping the trash can off at the curb when it gets there. One way to hold an object in place is with pressure and/or friction. Using two vertical conveyor belts, you could sandwich the trash can between two rollers. This would allow you to secure it in motion, then spin the rollers to release the can when you get to the curb. There are many ways using concepts explored with basic machines to solve engineering problems like this. Perhaps most importantly, there is no single right answer for designing a robot!

The design strategies in the example above focus on each individual aspect of a problem at a time. This can be critical for coming up with effective solutions to problems, especially when they are large and complicated in scope. For every engineering problem, you should be able to break down the mission into a number of constituent parts. This could result in a sort of linear approach in which you determine the importance of certain goals relative to others in the mission. In other words, you can dedicate more of the design focus to the primary aspects of the mission and leave peripheral issues for later in the design process. Another way to break up the task is to identify the ways in which multiple people could handle individual aspects of a robotics problem. If you know your robot will need a high-traction drive system as well as a lifting mechanism to complete its mission, it may be helpful to divide the creative labor among group members. It is important when doing this to note that both systems will inevitably be part of the same robotic assembly at some point down the line.

Part of designing with the big picture in mind comes with attention to detail and forethought for the integration of systems. If you have a claw assembly fully built and functional, but no good place to mount it on the robot's frame, then you could get

DESIGNING TIP

Designs should always have compatibility in mind. Try to break tasks down into smaller bits, but always keep in mind the bigger picture.

sent back to the drawing board in some cases. It's always good to look at the impact of your contribution to a robot's design. For instance, let's say your claw assembly is rather large and consequently heavy. Your team decides it's best to place the claw at the front of the robot based on its position relative to the objects the claw will manipulate. With all that weight at the front of the robot, the design team will have to find a way to counterbalance that weight with other components at the back of the robot. Sometimes a decision to mount an integral system will have certain consequences for other parts or mechanisms on the robot. In this example, it might be wise to store the robot's batteries on the back of the frame because they will have a good amount of weight to keep the robot balanced when it moves.

Solving Problems as a Team

One of the most important parts of problem solving in robotics is actually figuring out how to work with and address problems with other people. While movies and TV have probably shown you the antisocial mad scientist building robots alone in his lab, the reality of robot construction is far from that picture. A robot is really built when people get together to solve common goals and challenges using their expertise, motivation, and critical thinking. Working well with others can be paramount for ensuring the success of robotics projects as the designing, building, and troubleshooting phases all require cooperation among various parts of a team.

Starting with the design phase, brainstorming sessions need to be places where anyone can feel comfortable expressing his or her ideas. If a design session is dominated by a few aggressive individuals, it could mean that good ideas slip through the cracks during the meeting. If everyone at the table has an equal shot at bouncing ideas off the group, then you increase the diversity of methods and strategies for solving complex problems. As stated in the section above, there's no one way to build a robot, and sometimes, unconventional strategies prove to be the most effective for certain problems. Keeping an open mind can produce strong results, and making compromises is part of any collective effort.

Once the design and fabrication duties are divided among members of a group, it's important to develop good communication strategies. This could be something as simple as regular check-in meetings to see what progress each section of the group has made. During meeting sessions, it's good to ask what everyone currently needs to complete their task and identify areas where collaboration between subgroups will push the ball forward. For instance, if you have a design team and a build team, it can be critical to have sessions at which the preferred manufacturing methods of the build team are addressed in the design. The people who design a robot and the people who build it are not always the same. As a result, some technicians might have greater experience as to the way certain systems get wired or installed. Communication between parties can help prevent problems where designs fail to be actualized when tolerances between parts are too tight or pieces fit together differently than they did in computer simulations. If the design team can clearly communicate its ideas for connecting various systems, the entire team will have a much smoother time constructing the robot.

Robots also need some form of software and programming to run mechanical systems. In order for the programming team to be able to tackle control issues, it needs to be able to understand the constraints of the design and assembly of the machine. For instance, the physical position of sensors on the robot will necessarily have an impact on the data they gather for use in the program. Additionally, the power of moving components and speeds of various motors will largely determine how the software gets written. This is to say that the programmer must write commands for the microcontroller to send voltage to the electrical components on the robot. The amount of voltage and the interval at which it is applied is dependent on the electrical requirements of the system. If programmers have a clear picture of the limits of a robotic system, both physically and electrically, they will have a much better time implementing a solid coding strategy. Good control inherently comes from a good understanding of how the mechanisms function together in a system.

Robots in the Workplace and Safety

When professional engineers and technicians put together robots for a factory or manufacturing operation, they look at an immense number of considerations for design. They design these machines to make certain tasks much more efficient and safe for both operators and consumers. Let's take, for example, a machine that would be used to manufacture ballpoint pens. The question for these engineers is not limited only to "How do we make the most pens per minute?" They also must consider how the user will operate such a manufacturing machine. Even if the process is computer automated, manufacturing operations will have interfaces that allow line technicians to set parameters on the robotic processes. Such a machine should also be easily serviceable for a technician when parts need to be replaced. This means that the assemblies should be modular or easily accessible such that maintenance can be performed efficiently.

This type of build strategy identifies safety and ease of operation as primary concerns. Part of solving problems with robotics is being able to look at the practical application of the machines you design and build. Even if a robot performs its technical tasks of assembling or moving components incredibly well, it can still be poorly conceived if it doesn't cater to the needs of the people who use it. In other words, a robot that performs consistently but at the cost of safety and/or ease of operation fails to address one of the key questions of robotics projects: How does this machine help us? After all, what's the

Competitive robots should be equipped with safety features like guards around gear and chain assemblies.

point of a robot if it doesn't make things more manageable for us humans?

Part of building a great robot is making it safe to be around and operate. As a result, safety features often make up a good deal of the design process for machines with moving parts and forces that could be harmful. Both electrical and mechanical components should be safe to work on and be around. As a good example, robotics competitions often have a hardware inspection that goes over a number of criteria for safe operation on the field. On the inspection, you could see requirements like:

- Wires properly harnessed without risk of entanglement
- Electrical connections properly insulated/shielded to prevent fires or shorts
- Parts that move upon start-up should be labeled to protect students and referees
- All sharp corners and edges have been filed down or covered
- Main power switch labeled
- No components which could damage the field or other robots
- Potential pinch points should have guards or shields
- No flammable liquids or substances

This inspection checklist goes over a good range of general safety concerns for building robots. The truth of the matter is, robotic components like motors, actuators, and metal linkages are often more powerful than we are and can pose a risk of injury if proper safety measures are not taken. For example, sprockets and gears can be hazardous, especially to fingers poking around the robot. The point at which teeth mesh together or connect to a chain should be guarded to prevent such injuries. It is always helpful for such areas to be labeled for operators or technicians so they can be aware of mechanical dangers.

Sometimes safety measures need to be built in the environment around a robot instead of on the robot itself. On robotic assembly lines and manufacturing operations, engineers have come up with a number of good inventions to address safety concerns for workers. On some robotic CNC machines, sections of the floor in front of the machine are covered with pressure-sensitive pads. When a worker steps on the pad, the machine will immediately shut down and cease movement. As a safety feature, this addresses a need for an emergency cutoff system for times when something goes wrong with the machining process. Additionally, it ensures that humans can't step within a certain range of movement to be hit by the machine in certain positions.

Many automated manufacturing operations also have special safety features called **andon cords**. These cords are positioned in front of every part of the automated assembly process. When the cord gets pulled, the entire line shuts down. This can be a mechanism that allows operators to stop the line to address quality control issues or fix broken machines. Most importantly, these lines are available in the event that an operator experiences physically dangerous scenarios or, at worst, sustains a machine-related injury. These lines were famously used by Toyota in the car manufacturing lines as a safety

BRAIGO, THE ROBOTIC BRAILLE PRINTER

When Shubham Banerjee was just thirteen years old, he looked to robotics for a way to help people with visual impairments. Looking at the high cost of consumer braille printers, Shubham identified a need for a cheaper alternative. In order to satisfy this need, he began putting together a robot with LEGO pieces to take text files and convert them into physical characters on a roll of paper. Using a template for a drawing plotter with the LEGO Mindstorms system, he

Shubham Banerjee designed this revolutionary braille-printing robot.

set out to modify the mechanical aspects of the design to create the raised bumps on the paper. Thus, his invention, the Braigo, was born. The printing head works by putting small holes into the roll of paper as a mirror image of braille characters so that the raised bumps on the other side of the page read correctly for the user. Shubham set out to design the

Braigo with the user in mind. In order to do this, he placed a design constraint to build the robot using only parts from a single LEGO kit of parts. That way, the consumer could pick up the same product and build his or her own printer at a reasonable price.

In order to program the robot, Shubham wrote a script to translate the letters A–Z into their counterparts in braille. By uploading a piece of text into the microcontroller of the Braigo, the machine simply interprets the information letter by letter and arranges the six dotted configurations on the page. In order to move the print head around, he gave the printer three axes of movement. Using a motor to control each axis of movement (x, y, and z), Shubham programmed a set of motor movements to create the patterns of dots as the printer moves along the page.

Since his initial proof of concept was a resounding success, the Braigo V2 expands the robot's capabilities. Using an Intel Edison microcontroller in this new version, Shubham is moving from a do-it-yourself prototype to a production model. With the new control system, he has programmed the robot to do practical things such as printing the CNN headlines every morning for a user. This new version will be the very first cost-effective, silent, lightweight braille printer on the market.

feature and quality control measure. This mechanism addresses both safety and efficiency concerns simultaneously. Whenever a problem is encountered, the entire group can turn its attention to the issue with the stoppage of the entire assembly line.

Troubleshooting and Debugging

When a robot is fully assembled and programmed, it is actually far from complete. Solving problems extends well into the phase where your team is testing the robot for the first time and beyond. It is not a sign of poor design when you have to change things in your mechanical systems or programming. On the contrary, it's all part of the process of getting a design to its logical working form. The troubleshooting and debugging process involves a number of aspects, from isolating variables to trial and error.

Troubleshooting, more than anything, calls for a methodical process to produce good results. The first part of solving a problem is identifying its very root. The best way to do this is to form a hypothesis and test variables one at a time to get a definitive answer. This should sound very familiar from when you studied the scientific method in school. The process is exactly the same and should be documented so you have results to interpret and make informed decisions to move forward. Just as you would write up a lab report for an experiment, so too should you write down all your data and findings from robotic tests.

Let's look at a common example that could apply to many different robots. Say you power on your robot and everything looks fine except one of the motors doesn't move on a specific mechanism. The root of this problem could be electrical, mechanical, or code based, so it's time to start making hypotheses. Let's start with electrical because it has one of the most obvious places to look first. Is the motor plugged in? If not, then that's an easy fix! However, if it is indeed wired in, it's still possible that the electrical connection is insufficient. Starting with simple observations, you can look at the connections at the motor and the devices like speed controllers to which it may be hooked up.

Do the crimps or connectors look to be solidly in place? If they look good, it may be time to implement a more scientific test. One way to see if there's a good electrical connection is to test for **continuity** between two terminals on components. In order to test continuity, you need a device called a **multimeter**,

A technician checks resistance between components on a circuit board using a multimeter.

which allows you to check the resistance, voltage, and sometimes current of an electrical connection. By sending a very small charge through a wire with two probes attached to the multimeter, the device can be used to determine if the resistance between two terminals is small enough to be considered conductive. The ideal connection has zero resistance. Alternatively, a weak connection will read intermittently when jostled or have a high resistivity. Using the continuity test, you can also check if there is a short circuit in the electrical path to the motor. If the resistance between positive and negative terminals of a device is close to 0 ohms, then there is a short circuit that will damage components and prevent the motor from operating.

If all the electrical work checks out, you can look to see if the root of the motionless motor is mechanical in nature. Take a look at what the motor is doing. Is it lifting a heavy load? Is the attached component obstructed by anything? It is entirely possible that, even with the motor getting power, the load on the motor is too much for the motor's torque. This means that it doesn't have enough power to overcome the inertia to produce movement on an attached object that is providing force in the opposite direction of its rotation. For instance, if you have a fan motor small enough, you can probably stop it simply by putting your finger in the way of the plastic blades. The electrical current continues to flow to the fan, but the force provided by your finger is enough to prevent it from spinning. If the motor is indeed overburdened by a heavy load, then you can consider implementing a more powerful motor or looking at a higher gear ratio to increase the motor's torque.

TORQUE TIP

The smaller the gear attached to the motor relative to the one attached to the load, the more torque you get by reducing the velocity of the rotation on the load. The load will spin at a rate determined by the ratio of the two (or more) gears involved in a motor system.

Once you have eliminated the physical variables of electrical and mechanical issues, you can look to the realm of programming to find your answer. When commands are sent from a microcontroller to a motor (via a speed controller), the commands must be specified as a certain output. This means that there is a physical pin that carries the charge to the speed controller. This pin needs to be properly defined as the output for the given motor command in a program. In other words, the microcontroller's pin must be selected in the program so that it knows where to send the commands.

If all of your motors, inputs, and outputs are properly set up in the code, then you can look for errors in the **syntax** of the code. The syntax of a code language is essentially the set of rules and punctuation that you use to write lines of code. If the syntax is incorrect, the code will not work properly or as expected. It is very common to have systems not work simply because the programmers missed a single bit of punctuation in their code. Think of it like writing a regular essay in English. If you miss a period here and there, the reader will have a harder time following the meaning of your language. Sometimes, missing punctuation can completely obfuscate a whole paragraph or section when it is left out of critical places.

This small robot was put together using a microcontroller and motor assembly. Each pin needs to be properly identified in the coding.

The same goes for code. If the right punctuation is not given, the microcontroller won't be able to understand what you've written, potentially leading to unwanted commands or results.

Going through the code character by character is called debugging. The debugging process involves not only searching for errors but also finding ways to make the code run more smoothly. A good example of this is condensing functions of the code and removing redundancies. Going back to the example of writing an essay, you can see how writing the same sentence slightly differently over and over makes for an ineffective (and frankly, boring) text. The easier it is for the microcontroller to process your lines of code, the more quickly it will be able to run through the processes and produce movements on your robot.

Another part of debugging is changing values and variables in the code to test and get different results. Let's say you had the motor in question set to a speed of 10 percent. This value could be set as something like *motor_speed*, which is a variable.

This allows you to input whatever number you want within the given range of speeds and produce different movements from the motor. It's entirely possible that the 10 percent motor speed wasn't enough power to overcome the inertia of the load, just like we discussed above in the mechanical troubleshooting section. Raising the value to 40 percent motor power could be enough to solve the issue. This is where trial and error proves to be a solid method of tweaking values and getting the results that you want from the robot. Be sure to log all of your results so you have values to look back on if you decide to change it again in the future. Having this documentation will give you greater control by providing the team with a number of options for the robot's operation.

Conclusion

Problem solving is truly the nature of robotics in all facets of the process. Whether it's determining the mission for a robot or collaborating to fine-tune issues in the robot's operation, problem-solving strategies are an integral part of turning ideas and raw materials into moving machines. Teams of people must work together to achieve great things, especially in robotics, where multidisciplinary pursuits come together to form answers to complex problems. In this chapter, we have gone over how teams think about robots in terms of the problems they solve; the concerns they address, like safety and operation; and the issues they encounter along the way. Building a robot is most definitely a challenge for the brain to come up with creative solutions to problems both big and small.

A competition robot throws balls accurately into a goal from a distance.

5 The Motion of Humanoid Robots

So far, we have covered a range of topics in the field of robotics. From the elementary components of robots to their mechanical assembly and makeup, we explored general concepts and their potential application to a number of robotic systems. In this chapter, our goal is to examine a class of incredibly complex robots known as humanoids. They may actually be the robots you are most familiar seeing or reading about in popular media outlets. It's no surprise that we are so captivated by machines that look like us and can walk on two legs like we do. While the current capabilities of these robots fall short of some portrayals in science fiction, it is fascinating to look at advances in this field and what the potential implications may be in the future.

These kinds of robots are often on the cutting edge of various research fields in both hardware and software. As such, they are fantastic examples of some of the ways in which mechanical systems communicate and move together. Humanoid robots often build upon rudimentary concepts like motor and actuator control but implement them in ways that give feedback to every other part of a system. To show this in action, we will look at a few special robots that have been constructed to take on tasks that may seem basic to us humans but pose significant design challenges for robots.

In order to produce such incredible machines, robotics engineers and technicians also have to work on the cutting edge of processing and control techniques. They must often use computers to aid their design and construction process to get maximum precision from their materials. We will look at the integral role computer processing plays in the way robots understand information. This will give us a more comprehensive understanding of the information that they use and the ways that artificial intelligence is implemented.

Humanoid robots also have a lot to offer us in terms of the work they could do for us and with us in everyday life. Part of this chapter will look at the way that different humanoid systems are designed to suit different needs or projects. There are so many applications, from human interaction to manual labor, and each prompts different construction techniques and robot agility requirements. A robot built to work in a warehouse will be very different than one that is built to provide care and companionship in the home. We will take a look at the way different technologies are implemented to achieve certain goals through research and development.

Robots That Can Play Catch

Imagine if someone came to you and asked you to build a robot that could catch a ball that was thrown at it. What would this kind of task entail mechanically? How could the robot see or follow the ball? What kind of device would you use to grab it? If these questions seem daunting, don't worry, they should. Engineers and computer scientists have been grappling with this challenge for years. To make matters even more interesting, one particular humanoid robot has been constructed to catch thrown objects the way that we do as humans. In other words, this robot watches the ball in flight, anticipates its movement, and moves its hand into position to catch a ball at exactly the right moment in time. While such a task is one of the first things some of us learn to do as children, it calls for many complex control methods for robots. It is not at all straightforward to think of the ways to replicate every part of the process we humans go through to throw and catch a ball. Let's break down some of the ways that researchers have tackled these problems.

This particular humanoid robot is named **"Rollin' Justin."** Justin was developed by the German Aerospace Center to perform a number of tasks using its incredibly dexterous torso and arms. The aerospace program designed this robot to be able to work on satellites in space using human control from Earth. "Rollin' Justin" is a variation created for terrestrial tests and applications that require a mobile system as a base. It gets the name "Rollin' Justin" from its four-wheeled drive system that helps it move between tasks. Each wheel has its own spring suspension system that can move independently of its upper body. This feature allows the robot to drive around in any direction and keep its focus on objects or obstacles in front of it. Additionally, the suspension can be adjusted to change how

The highly advanced robot Justin interacting with German chancellor Angela Merkel using the actuators in its hands

close or far the wheels are to or from the body. This means that the robot can pull the wheels in to drive through narrow spaces or spread them out to gain balance if needed.

The "Rollin'" part of Justin plays one of many roles in order to achieve its goals. Justin's arms are constructed to be able to move in nearly any possible articulation as would a normal human arm. This is important for the human control interface, which has users manipulate arm and hand controls from a distant location. Since the arms can move naturally the way the user's arms would, motions can be both intuitive and fluid when taking control of the robot. Justin's upper body has, in total, 43 degrees of freedom that can be controlled by a user. This means that natural movements can be replicated by mechanical joints all over the torso, head, and arms.

Justin's hands are particularly noteworthy. While they are about 50 percent larger than an average pair of human hands, these robotic hands possess an astonishing amount of fine motor skills. Pressure sensors in the fingers give feedback to the robot's microcontroller, which the user can utilize to see how firmly or softly to grab an object. One truly amazing feature is the use of **torque sensors** in the motors of the arms. These can set and remember specific positions for various tasks. Your normal human grip works in very similar ways with muscle memory. Think about when you reach for a cup of water. Before even placing your fingers around the cup, your body knows how much force to apply to be able to pick it up without crushing or dropping it. Moreover, you probably (if even subconsciously) change the amount of pressure on a cup based on whether it's made of paper, plastic, or Styrofoam. Justin's hands work exactly in this way so they can not only pick up objects but "remember" the force it took by saving the torque information to the robot's hard drive.

Because of this incredibly fine control of the hands and fingers, Justin can perform tasks that are very complex for robots. Take, for instance, the action of opening a jar. While it's something we do without giving any thought, an incredible amount of fine motion and control goes into it. Think of every position and movement as another instance of programming and robot control and you can begin to break down the steps it would take for Justin to open such a jar. First, the robot picks up the jar with one hand, looks at it, then determines how the other hand should proceed. It is important that every motion involving two hands is performed such that there is no collision between them. As a result, Justin is programmed to plot a course that avoids obstacles and collisions on its way to the lid of the jar. Once there, the fingers have to press down around the lid, then move in a rolling motion to unscrew it from the jar. It takes multiple rotations to get the lid completely off given that Justin's wrists, like ours, are limited to a certain degree of rotational motion.

There is yet another element that underlies this kind of complex motion. You may have heard of your body's sixth sense. This is thought of as the sense that allows you to know where your limbs are in relation to each other. This, too, has to be programmed in Justin in order to keep the distance between two hands relative to each other for certain tasks. The developers use a concept called "**spatial impedance**" to place constraints between certain mechanical systems. This means that the hands are impeded or prevented from extending beyond an area in space. This is important when you think of picking up or manipulating objects with both of your hands. If you were to pick up a trash can two-handed, the space between your hands would need to stay constant to keep your grip on the can. No matter how your elbows, shoulders, or wrists move, the hands need to have spatial impedance to hold an object and move it around.

Justin "Sees" the Ball

Another one of Justin's many feats is its ability to measure distance and track movement of objects. This robot's head has two "eyes" made up of high-definition cameras. Robots have to be given a way to interpret video data into meaningful information. Without a way to translate the information for the vision processor, the video is really just light captured by the camera and represented as pixels. As a result, software developers have to sort pixels from each other to give a robot **object recognition**. Again, this is something that we humans do without a thought. We see a table, and every object on top of it appears to be discrete based on color, shape, texture, etc. In order to give robots the same sense, we have to define a number of constraints to sort objects from one another.

Object recognition is a very advanced field of software and robotics but is implemented in lots of commercial technology. Ever notice the little square that pops up on your digital camera around people's faces? Facial recognition is one of the many forms that has its own criteria to determine the parts of a picture that are and are not faces. Justin's cameras are constantly working to define objects that are significant to its tasks and operations. The vision processor looks at two models of object classification: **symbolic** and **geometric recognition**. These methods are informed by any stored information on the robot as part of a strategy for how to manipulate the object. For instance, when Justin sees a jar with a lid, the robot takes into account the symbolic association between the object and a scheme of actions to unscrew it. Additionally, Justin must assess the geometric properties of the object to identify specific dimensions to handle the present task at hand.

These two models work hand in hand to determine a hierarchy of motion. This means that the robot has a number of different pieces of information to use at any given moment of processing and motion planning. This hierarchy determines the value of information in the system and sorts it based on certain priorities for a given action. In other words, the fact that the jar has a lid needs to be addressed before the robot reaches for the geometric object in order to effectively open it. Without a prior scheme for how to classify the object symbolically, the robot would have a significantly harder time getting to the right course of action.

An Overview of Object Recognition

When it comes to object recognition in general, computers mostly rely on their ability to define objects by their outlines or edges. If you think about it, we do the same thing for the most part when we look at the edges of an object to see where it ends and another object begins. For identifying outlines in digital images, there are two main classes of vision processing: appearance-based methods and feature-based methods. These processes are best explained through examples, so here are a number of common functions for each.

Appearance-based methods often use a process of comparing and contrasting imagery. When the computer is loaded with example images, it analyzes a frame of the video and looks for matches in a database of pictures. These example images or templates are used to calculate variance between the two images being compared. The computer can then look for differences in color, lighting, and perspective to approximate the transformation of an object from the template to the image from the camera. The more templates you have for an object, the more accurately the computer can identify that object.

It can be important when performing image processing to reduce the amount of information you need to identify objects. Certain kinds of **edge detection** make processing more efficient by defining objects in terms of their edges and consequently ignoring the rest of the information. One such method is called canny edge detection. This process starts by smoothing the resolution of the image so that noise in the picture is not construed as a false edge. This prevents the computer from identifying things as objects that aren't objects at all. You've probably seen your camera put a box around an object that wasn't relevant to the picture you were trying to take. This means that the noise in the image produced a false positive for the image processor. The detection process then looks at points of intensity gradients. This means that the difference in light value between two objects in the image is measured and the direction of the outline is determined by the program.

An image of a flower is depicted in canny edge detection.

The second method of image processing is feature based. This method also uses templates to compare images and find matches, but it is focused on a different set of criteria. Objects in templates are further classified into features, which can be things like distinct surfaces, edges, or corners. When a certain number of features in an image correspond to the features in a template, the program recognizes the object as a match. In order to do this, the computer must make a hypothesis to test whether a set of features produces a match. This hypothesis is then tested to confirm or deny the identity of an object based on a database. The tests can be run on the **pose** or orientation and position of features. Hypotheses can also be tested using geometric correlation between template and image features.

While this is hardly an exhaustive account of the way that software engineers sort through images on a robot, it should give you a good idea about the complexity of the problem. Image processing and object recognition are often *very* processor intensive, meaning that the robot or computer must dedicate a lot of power to the task. This is an incredibly powerful tool for a number of applications in robotics at all levels. The truth is, most of the object recognition legwork has already been done in a number of coding languages popular in robotics. Camera integration and image processing are complicated subjects but are hardly arcane in their applications.

Justin Follows the Ball

So Justin has identified the object as a ball and it's now hurtling through the air. What happens next? How does the robot calculate the path of the ball in flight? How can it tell the speed of the ball to react in time? The answer is a complex combination of sensors, motors, and algorithms. Inside Justin's head, the two high-definition cameras provide a stereo image. In other words, they are placed at a fixed position in the head,

Stereoscopic vision places the subjects of the image in different parts of the frame, allowing for distance calculations. A stereoscope creates a 3-D image.

separated by a given distance. This is the same as the way your eyes provide you with a stereo image of the world, giving you a composite of two similar perspectives. Our **stereoscopic vision** allows us to perceive objects in three dimensions, or in other words, to perceive depth. Depth perception is an integral part of our ability to throw, catch, or judge distances of objects in motion.

In order for Justin to make use of this stereo imagery, the developers had to figure out a way to assess the differences in perspective between the two cameras. In other words, when the ball is thrown, at any given position, it will show up in different parts of the frame for each of the two cameras. Using this information, you can triangulate the distance between the two perspectives and the object. If you consider the two cameras and a moving object to be three points of a polygon, you can think of the relationship between them as a triangle. Given that the distance between the two cameras will always be the same, you can assess the distance of the object in terms of the angles of the triangle. In other words, the position of the object in each frame can be expressed as an angle that can be used to calculate the entire triangle. Using simple trigonometry, you can use the length of the side between the cameras and the measurements of all the angles to give you the length of the two missing sides.

Harnessing the Speed of Light

In order to judge the distance away of moving objects, Justin is also equipped with a special sensor called a photonic mixer device, or PMD. This device acts as a **time-of-flight camera** by shooting a light signal at an object and then receiving that signal back on a focal plane array. While it can be used to measure the distance of flying objects, the term "time of flight" actually refers to the amount of time it takes the light particles to fly through the air and back. The PMD shoots a light signal that is turned on and off or modulated at a certain frequency. Since the PMD has a reference for the phase of the outgoing and incoming light signals, it can calculate the discrepancy in phase between them. In other words, the sensor uses the constant of the speed of light to calculate the position of an object based on the reported phase of the modulated light signal.

The PMD fires a broad signal and receives varying distances of reflections on the different points of the receiving

MATH MOMENT

Here's an example of how Justin measures distance. Say there is a ball on the table in front of two cameras that are spaced 2 feet (0.6 m) apart. In the left camera, the ball is 15 degrees right of center on the frame. For the camera on the right, the ball appears 30 degrees to the left of center on the frame. When you think of this problem as a triangle, you should consider the center of each frame on the cameras to be 90 degrees. In other words, the angles would be (90 – 15 = 75) for the left camera and (90 – 30 = 60) for the one on the right. With this information, we are equipped to figure out the remaining dimensions of the triangle. The angles of every triangle add up to a total of 180 degrees, so to get the third angle, we have to do some subtraction. The remaining angle would be 180 – 75(L) – 60(R) = 45 degrees. We can then use the law of sines to find the distance from each camera. The law of sines says the length of one side of a triangle divided by the sine of the opposite angle yields the same quotient for each side. Using the equation $a/\sin(75°) = 2/\sin(45°)$, we can solve for the side "a" on the triangle. Let's redistribute the equation to: $a = [2 \times \sin(75°)]/\sin(45°) = 2.732$ feet (0.833 m) from the right camera. Now that we have side "a," we can perform the same calculation to get the remaining side: $b = [2 \times \sin(60°)]/\sin(45°) = 2.449$ feet (0.746 m) from the left camera.

A robot like Rollin' Justin will triangulate the position of an object many times in a single second. This allows the onboard computer to determine the trajectory of a moving object. The more information the robot has about the position of the object through the air in time, the more

Outfielders calibrate their movements to follow the trajectory of a fly ball. They hope to reach the ball's landing spot before the ball does.

accurately it can predict where to extend its hand to catch it. We tend to process incoming moving objects in a very similar way. When an object is first in flight, it can be hard to tell exactly where it will land. Think of a baseball player going after a fly ball. The player may start by running in a very general direction when the ball is hit. It is only after the ball has been in flight for some time that the player begins to make small adjustments to his path to intercept the ball. This is the product of taking in lots of information about the position of the ball as it flies through the air.

An Xbox Kinect uses time-of-flight cameras to track the motion of participants during gameplay.

focal plane. This means that objects at different distances will reflect back to different parts of the array, creating an image comprised of different values for depth. This, in turn, creates an array of pixels out of the data that shows the depth of objects in an entire scene. Commercial products have also begun to use this advanced technology. In fact, the second generation Kinect for the Xbox One uses a time-of-flight camera to provide real-time movement tracking for interactive gaming. This allows for recognition not only of human movement but of more complex, depth-oriented gestures.

Good Catch! Now Throw It Back!

All of the systems explored above play an integral role in the process of getting a humanoid robot to consistently catch a ball. It's pretty unbelievable to consider the amount of high-level thinking and problem solving involved in a task we humans consider to be very basic. Within the past few years, however, the German Aerospace Center has developed the design further to increase its capabilities. This newer version is called "Agile Justin" and features a number of innovations. Primarily, this robot is faster. The developers improved the mechanical gear ratios of the motors in the upper body of the robot, making the limbs much more agile. What this means, in reality, is that the new and improved robot can use its whole body to throw the ball to a specific location.

This shows the process of troubleshooting, improvement, and innovation at a very high level. Research in humanoid robotics is often pushing new boundaries like this. While you might think that the ability to throw a ball might not be all that consequential, it's actually the general agility and dexterity that should be a cause for excitement. In other words, throwing a ball is really just an indicator that the robot could perform many actions more quickly and efficiently. This could mean more efficient repairs in space or simply greater capabilities as a test platform for robotic problem solving. These kinds of advancements should be viewed largely in the context of their potential. This is to say that the application of Justin as a test platform could mean great things for important practical applications in the real world.

Humanoids with a Different Purpose

We've just taken a look at a humanoid robot that was designed to test the capabilities of fine motor skills and articulation. Justin is just one of many humanoids out there for the purpose of research and development in the field of robotics. It is important to note that every humanoid robot is usually designed to guide a different strain of research or inquiry. In this section, we'll look at some other popular humanoid robots and their contributions to robotics. Humans can move in many complex ways that extend beyond the reach of mechanical movement currently. Each of these robots will be an exploration into different facets of the movement of the human body.

Boston Dynamics and Atlas

Boston Dynamics is an American robotics research institute that focuses on the task of getting robots to walk. Over the years, they have developed a number of quadrupedal (four-legged) and bipedal (two-legged) robots to exhibit the mechanics of walking and traversing uneven terrain. Their most recent addition to the robot family is called **Atlas** and is particularly gifted at walking and balancing on two legs. Atlas is powered with an electrical tether, but its movements are actuated by hydraulic cylinders. Hydraulics provide a lot of force and are good for this application given that the aluminum and titanium robot weighs a whopping 330 pounds (150 kilograms). Similar to Justin, Atlas uses two stereo imaging cameras and a laser device to measure distance. The **laser range finder (LFR)** uses a single laser beam to determine

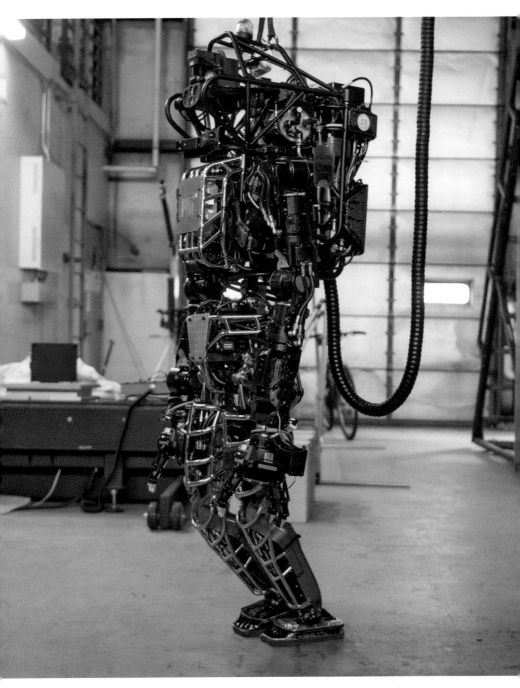

The humanoid robot Atlas walks upright with a complex system of sensors, motors, and algorithms.

the distance from an object (in this case, the ground relative to the robot). It is based on the same principle as time-of-flight cameras but only processes the distance from a single beam of light from the laser.

Atlas's most impressive feat is walking outside through rough terrain without losing balance. In fact, this robot has traversed areas of snowy woods and stayed on its own two legs. Even as agile human beings, we can be susceptible to slipping and falling in the snow, so it is no small task to ask of a robot. This robot also has the ability to recover from significant disturbances when walking. During tests, technicians will go up to Atlas and kick the robot to try to make it fall over. The robot will stumble, but it catches its balance and continues on its path. The same kind of recovery function can be seen in other aspects of the robot as well. When carrying a package or payload as part of an autonomous program, the package can be completely knocked out of the hands of the robot. Atlas then locates the package with object recognition and goes to pick it back up and continue on. This kind of resilient programming makes for very capable robots that can carry out tasks in spite of tough obstacles.

This robot was developed as a part of the Defense Advanced Research Projects Agency, or DARPA, to provide disaster relief capabilities. As such, the purpose of the robot was to be able to walk across rubble and wreckage to assist survivors of disasters both natural and otherwise. Among its capabilities are operating hand power tools, opening doors, and even driving a car. The DARPA robotics challenge was inspired by the Fukushima Daiichi Nuclear Power Plant disaster. Based on the idea that robots can withstand levels of radiation that are deadly to humans, this robotics competition seeks to provide mechanical solutions to unthinkable tragedies. Atlas was created as an entry to this competition and in 2015 came in second place by completing all eight challenges of a simulated disaster environment.

ASIMO

ASIMO is a robot developed by Honda with a very different set of goals in mind. Its name is an acronym for Advanced Step in Innovative Mobility, and it serves to move around in human environments. A much smaller robot of only 51 inches (130 cm) and 110 pounds (50 kg), ASIMO was designed not only to perform certain functions but to have a particular look. The stout height of this robot was actually researched and determined to be smaller than the average human but tall enough to reach light switches and doorknobs. This robot is intended to be a robotic assistant for humans and focuses on movement in terms of interaction.

Much of ASIMO's vision processing is used to create a sense of attention and interaction between the robot and a human. The stereoscopic cameras in the head of the robot are programmed to recognize and follow faces. Moreover, this vision processing is used to identify gestures and postures to be able to respond to various situations with a human counterpart. In fact, this robot has been programmed to recognize and perform a handshake as well as turn to follow the sound of someone calling its name. ASIMO uses voice control and recognition to determine whether a person is a companion, with the ability to recognize and store up to ten different voices and people. In fact, the robot has eight microphones that allow it to simultaneously pick up signals from multiple sources without any trouble.

In addition to ASIMO's ability to recognize human interactions, the robot can also display a range of different responses both verbally and visually. This robot can ask you what you would like to drink, say your order back to you, then go fetch the drink on its own. The artificial intelligence of this machine is truly remarkable. The AI on board allows ASIMO to adapt to situations and autonomously make decisions without any human command or control. In fact, ASIMO will politely sidestep any humans that it walks in front of. Additionally, if the robot's batteries are low, it will autonomously walk over to its charging station and plug itself back in.

There are many bipedal humanoid robots that can walk, but very few that can run. ASIMO can actually run at speeds of nearly 4 miles per hour (6.4 kilometers per hour). This is a particularly daunting task for a robot because of the times in between steps in which the robot is completely off the ground. This means that it loses the feedback from its legs and must rely on balancing algorithms as well as readings from the distance sensors to keep going. For this, ASIMO has two **ultrasonic sensors** that use sound waves to calculate distance to the floor from the waist of the robot. With one sensor on the front, and one at the base of the robot's backpack, ASIMO has comprehensive control over bipedal motion and balance.

As you can see, ASIMO is a very different kind of robot with very different kinds of goals in mind. One of the robotics engineers behind ASIMO is Satoshi Shigemi. He outlined the project of Honda's robot in an interview, saying, "From the

ASIMO brings joy to children by interacting and dancing, while not getting in their way.

beginning we wanted to design a robot that could help people. To realize that dream we are constantly asking ourselves what kind of robot would be able to change society, make people happy, and make life easier for people around the world." This is a kind of problem solving that is very large in scope but calls for very interesting advances in robotics. Moving into the future, it's easy to see how interactions between humans and robots will only become more important, and ASIMO is certainly leading the way.

Conclusion

In this chapter, we took a glimpse into the world of advanced humanoid robots and how they work. Even though they are machines of tremendous complexity, they can still be defined largely in terms of moving parts and the sensors that give them control. Humanoid robots have a lot to teach us about the capabilities of machines as well as the difficulties of recreating human motion. This field is both humbling and inspiring, revealing how far robotics has come and how much we have left to uncover.

This book covered a large range of topics, starting very basic and building toward the implementation of many systems working as a robotic ensemble. Hopefully you've been able to see how robotics could play a bigger role in your own life. Whether you're inspired to get involved making your own moving parts or you have simply gained understanding for the robots that shape your everyday experience, you can now identify the ways in which you can relate to robots, and the process that creates them.

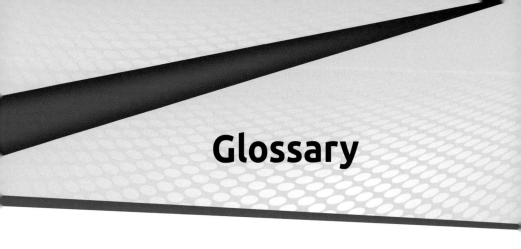

Glossary

ABS plastic Plastic with low melting temperature used for fabrication and 3-D printing.

andon cords Safety features in mechanical assembly lines used to halt production and address a particular problem.

ASIMO A humanoid robot with artificial intelligence developed by Honda to be a human companion.

Atlas A bipedal humanoid robot developed by Boston Dynamics to compete in the DARPA robotics challenge.

axes of articulation Moving system consisting of two or more joints or linkages that allow a mechanism to move in multiple three-dimensional planes.

brushless DC motor An electric motor that rapidly switches between energized coils to produce the rotation of a rotor.

cable carrier A movable wire management system consisting of segmented housing linkages.

cam A mechanism that translates rotational motion into linear motion or vice versa using a spinning or sliding constraint.

carbon fiber Expensive composite material made from woven carbon strands cured into sheets and three-dimensional shapes using epoxy or resin.

center of gravity The point at which all gravitational forces on an object are equal, providing the most balance.

clockwork motor A motor that rotates from the stored energy of a wound spring.

commutator Conductor that makes an electrical connection to a rotating object with some kind of constant applied force.

continuity Sufficient conductivity between two terminals along a wire or circuit.

C-rate A measurement of how long it takes the battery to discharge based on its capacity and current flow.

crimps Electrical connectors used to terminate wires and attach various components in a circuit.

debugging Process of troubleshooting for programming to get expected outputs from a given input.

Delrin Low-friction machinable plastic used commonly in sliding mechanisms.

edge detection Process of identifying outlines of objects based on distinct features in a picture or video.

80-20 Extruded aluminum tubing with channels for mounting, sliding, or structural linkages.

electromagnetic interference (EMI) External disturbance to an electrical signal or circuit that reduces quality and fidelity of that signal.

feedback Electrical signal sent from a sensor to a microcontroller giving information about status or position.

geometric recognition Matching of constituent parts based on their relation to geometric shapes found in matching images.

heatshrink Insulating tube material that shrinks down to the outside of a wire when a heat threshold is exceeded.

heatsink A device that protects electronics by transferring excess heat from components so it can be cooled by fans or moving fluids.

inclined plane A tilted material or surface that uses the potential energy from gravity to move objects.

kinematics The field of classical mechanics for studying the relationship between two or more constrained objects in a moving system.

laser range finder (LRF) A device that measures the distance from a surface or object by capturing a reflected laser beam and calculating based on the constant speed of light.

lead screw A mechanism using physical constraints to produce linear motion actuated by the rotating threads of a screw.

lever A rigid section of material that pivots at a fulcrum.

limit switch An electromechanical device that switches an electrical signal when touched by an object or frame component.

linear actuator A mechanism that moves forward or backward in a straight line due to pressure in an enclosed cylinder or mechanical translation from a rotating motion.

LiPo battery Lithium polymer battery that is rechargeable and consists of individual cells that allow for large amounts of power in a small form factor.

locomotion Movement or transportation from one location to another.

multimeter An electrical measurement device that can read voltage, resistance, amperage, and sometimes more.

object recognition Algorithmic gathering of data from video and images that looks for matches of stored objects from a database.

omni wheels Wheels comprised of a number of rollers that surround the circumference of the wheel, allowing for movement perpendicular to the wheel's direction.

pneumatic motor A motor which uses directional air pressure to produce mechanical rotation.

pose Position of an object based on the perspective of a robot's camera(s).

primary batteries Batteries that are chemically altered when discharged, which makes them single-time use.

pulley Wheel and axle used to support tension or weight by changing the direction of a cable or rope.

Rollin' Justin A robot developed by the German Aerospace Center as a platform for research in humanoid robotic movement.

rotor Moving component of an electric motor that produces rotation from windings that interact with magnetic fields.

slip ring A device that creates an electrical connection from a rotating object to a stationary structure using commutators.

spatial impedance An advanced robotics concept that constrains two moving arm systems at a fixed distance for object manipulation.

stator Stationary component of an electric motor that is responsible for the alignment of the electromagnetic field.

stereoscopic vision Usage of multiple cameras (or eyes) to provide sense of depth and calculate distance of objects in three dimensions.

strain relief Controlled point of tension on wires to ease stress on electrical connections and components.

symbolic recognition Identification of objects on a systematic basis in terms of their relation to other objects or moving parts.

syntax The set of rules and punctuation used to write lines of code in a given programming language.

tank drive Drive system using two sets of wheels or tracks which spin in opposite directions to turn or pivot.

time-of-flight camera A camera that measures how long it takes a pulse of light to leave the camera, reflect off an object, and return. Using the constant speed of light, it can calculate the distance to the object and provide calculations for the movement of the object.

timing belt A belt with evenly spaced teeth to mesh with a gear to translate rotational movement across a given distance without slippage.

torque sensor A device that measures the force on a rotational mechanism for use by a microcontroller.

treads Continuous sections of tracks linked around wheels to provide large amounts of traction and control.

ultrasonic sensor A device that calculates distance by sending out high-frequency sound waves and measuring the time it takes them to travel back to a microphone on the sensor.

wedge A triangular object used for the separation of objects or parts from an object, lifting, or holding an object stationary.

wheel and axle Assembly that translates rotational motion from a shaft to a wheel of larger diameter and vice versa.

work hardening Property that makes a material more brittle over time through stress and movement.

zip tie A ratcheting fastener used to secure bundles of wires together or to structural components.

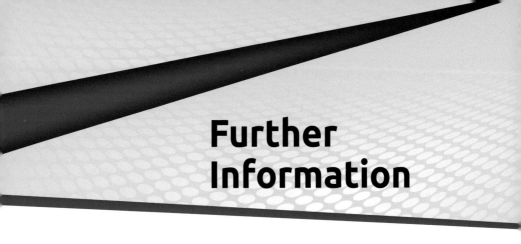

Further Information

Competition Websites

Botball

www.botball.org

Botball is a competitive robotics platform for autonomous robots only. Botball robots utilize the C programming language to perform their autonomous runs.

FIRST Robotic Competition

www.firstinspires.org

This site is the clearinghouse for all FIRST competitions from Jr. FLL to FRC. You can find rules, registration, and area event information here.

High Tech Kids

www.hightechkids.org

This site, run by volunteers in the state of Minnesota, provides free resources and training for teams competing in FLL and other competitions.

Robotics Education and Competition Foundation

www.roboticseducation.org

The Robotics Education and Competition Foundation provides two separate competitions for VEX IQ and VEX EDR robots.

World Robot Olympiad

www.wroboto.org

The World Robot Olympiad is a yearly competition that has dance, football (soccer), and search and rescue categories.

Instructional Websites

Chief Delphi

www.chiefdelphi.com

These forums are a great resource to connect with other FIRST Robotics teams. There is also a lot of useful information for general robotics, design, and programming.

Damien Kee's Technology in Education Page

www.damienkee.com

Damien Kee has been a leader in educational robotics for over a decade now. He has written several books on robotics, and his design for Riley Rover is used in hundreds of classrooms around the world. You should join his robotics email group (sign up from his site).

GITHub

github.com

GitHub is a collaboration tool for the programming and web design team. The site allows you to upload and work on code in various languages without altering the format. Use this tool to divide up different programming tasks and conquer!

Instructables

www.instructables.com

A haven for all things DIY, Instructables provides a place for users to show off their projects with step-by-step breakdowns. Can be very useful when looking for inspiration on how to tackle a new project.

LEGO Engineering

www.legoengineering.com

Hosted by Tufts University Center for Engineering Education and Outreach (CEEO), this site contains hundreds of articles pertaining to the world of robotics education.

Make Magazine

www.youtube.com/user/makemagazine/ playlists?sort=dd&view=1

Make Magazine has a very active YouTube channel with tons of interesting content. In particular, the "Colin's Lab" series of videos can teach you a lot about circuits.

MIT

ocw.mit.edu/index.htm

The Massachusetts Institute of Technology offers free courses online in a huge range of fields. While definitely for the ambitious student, these courses present immense amounts of useful theory for robotics applications.

Pneumatics Online

www.pneumaticsonline.com/calculator.htm

This website is great for calculating requirements for pneumatic cylinders and actuators on your robot. The calculator can also be used to check your work after doing the calculations by hand in the shop.

Sparkfun Electronics

www.sparkfun.com
This website is great for getting into circuits or finding electronics and sensors for your robot.

Product Websites

AndyMark

www.andymark.com
AndyMark is a robotics part supplier with many good options for motors, actuators, servos, etc. AndyMark is a sponsor of FIRST Robotics and supplies many of the items in the kit of parts.

DigiKey

www.digikey.com
DigiKey is an online electronics superstore. If you're building circuits and need resistors, capacitors, transistors, etc., DigiKey is good for getting what you need quickly. They have a mind-numbing number of components, so try not to get lost!

Mindsensors

www.mindsensors.com
One of the companies that makes third-party sensors for EV3 robots, including a line of cameras.

VEX Robotics

www.vexrobotics.com
VEX has a robotic system of modular building parts for ease of construction. They sell both kits and parts for competition robots.

Index

Page numbers in **boldface** are illustrations. Entries in **boldface** are glossary terms.

About the Author

Kevin McCombs works as a research and development technician at a drone company based in Jacksonville, Florida. He has a bachelor's degree from New College of Florida in philosophy and music. With ten years' experience building competition robots, he is a mentor and volunteer at his brother's nonprofit, which expands youth robotics in north Florida. The organization has facilitated the growth of more than 150 robotics teams in the area, with the hopes of putting a team in every public school. In his free time, when he isn't making machines and circuits, Kevin plays lead guitar in a death metal band and works as a mixing engineer for local music groups. Whether it's robotics or music, Kevin just likes working with metal.